The Musée D'ORSAY

© 2007 by SCALA Group S.p.A., Florence
© 2007 Publishing Project: E-ducation.it, Florence

This 2007 edition published by Barnes & Noble, Inc. by
arrangement with SCALA Group S.p.A.

Project Director: Cinzia Caiazzo
Editor-in-chief: Filippo Melli
Texts: Margherita d'Ayala Valva
Scientific Advice: Chiara Piccinini
Editorial Staff: Giulia Marrucchi; Francesca Bianchi,
Vanessa Gavioli, Carolina Orlandini
Graphic design: Edimedia; Stefania Laudisa
Translation: Shanti Evans

© Photographs: SCALA Group Photographic Archives,
Florence
except for:
© SCALAGROUP and COREL All rights reserved
© PLANET ART, Beverly Hills CA

Illustrations, selected from the Scala Archives, of property
belonging to the Italian Republic are published by
concession of the competent authority (Ministero per i
Beni e le Attività Culturali).

ISBN-13: 978-0-7607-9441-8
ISBN-10: 0-7607-9441-3

Printed and bound in China, 2007

1 3 5 7 9 10 8 6 4 2

The Musée D'ORSAY

BARNES & NOBLE

NEW YORK

Contents

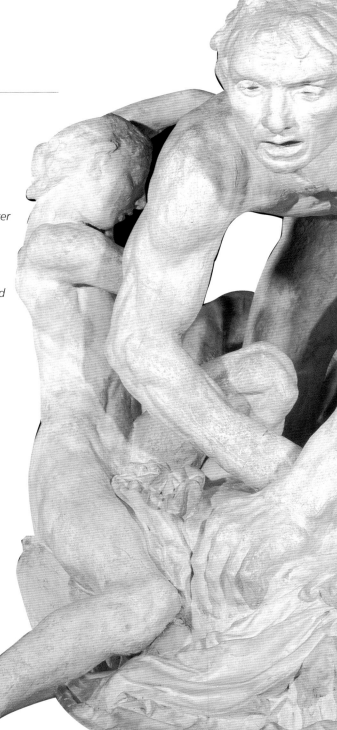

Masterpieces of the Nineteenth Century in a Railstation

Imagine taking a leap into the past and finding yourself right in the middle of a railroad station, over a century ago. This station, the Gare d'Orsay, has just been opened, to coincide with the World Exposition of 1900. Every device or mechanism in operation, every clerk or worker involved in running the place, is a reflection of the efficiency and faith in progress that are characteristics of the age. This building and its attached hotel, constructed to receive and accommodate travelers arriving in the heart of Paris from the southwest of Europe, are designed to meet requirements that are at once functional and aesthetic. It is worth remembering that the station has risen from the ashes of the Cour des Comptes (Court of Accounts), whose architects had been rash enough to claim that it «has been constructed out of totally fireproof materials»: unfortunately the revolutionaries of the Commune, who evidently had not been told about this, burned it down in 1871. Such a precedent helps to explain the imposing appearance of the station building, its size and its functional character: the architect, Victor Laloux, used the most typical materials of his day – the iron of the Eiffel Tower and the glass of the Crystal Palace in London – to create the core of a structure (then clad with stone) which was considered absolutely modern and indestructible. "The need to come and go freely," wrote Laloux, "is clearly expressed today by the masses, who have a horror of waiting in line, a horror of narrow passageways and dark corners, a horror above all of everything that might constitute an obstacle to the free dispersal of a crowd emerging from a hall or a train," and so the exit from the station leads into an open space. So picture yourself in the midst of this crowd of elegantly dressed people in a hurry to get to their destination, but who are entranced, on emerging from the station, by the sight of the banks of the Seine.

Now come back to earth and walk through the great central hall of the Orsay Museum: you will find that you are on approximately the same level as the old tracks, but surrounded now by sculptures

in the eclectic style of the second half of the 19th century. On your left there are the rooms devoted to the legacy of the great figures of the academy (Ingres and the *Ingresques*) and romanticism (Delacroix, Chassériau). On your right, the walls of the rooms are covered with the huge works of Courbet and the masters of realism. Continuing your tour of the museum's three different levels, you will be able to follow the evolution of Western art during a period of exceptional ferment, which saw the birth of impressionism and its eclipse by so-called postimpressionism, and the emergence of naturalistic and symbolist currents at the official exhibitions (the Salons): the period extends from 1848 to around 1905 for painting, and up to 1914 for other sectors of art. In fact "all" the visual arts of the second half of the 19th century are covered in the museum: from the genres traditionally represented in the Louvre – painting, sculpture, the decorative arts (objects and furniture) and drawing – to the graphic arts (printing and photography), architecture, city planning and cinematography, the last invention of a century that has been described as "a speculator in the image business."

But where did the strange idea of turning a railroad station into a museum come from? We have to go back to 1977 when, following the transfer of the collections of 20th-century art to the Centre Georges Pompidou (known as the Beaubourg), an entire period in the history of art remained excluded, or almost, from public view: the scarcity of space at the Musée du Jeu de Paume (the museum of the impressionists) meant that many masterpieces were kept in storage, along with a whole group of pictures

and sculptures in the Louvre that, despite their reassessment by critics at the time, did not fall into any of the chronological or aesthetic categories applied at either the Louvre or the Beaubourg. In the meantime, a disused construction in the heart of Paris had been slated for demolition to make room

▲ **JEAN-BAPTISTE CARPEAUX,** *Four Quarters of the World,* 1890.

▶ **THOMAS COUTURE,** *The Romans of the Decadence,* 1847.

for a hotel; but the Parisians, already unhappy about the recent razing of the 19th-century markets (Les Halles), were not willing to countenance its destruction. This was, in fact, the station built by Laloux in 1900 and abandoned in 1939. Thus the idea of saving the complex of the station and its hotel coincided with the search for a suitable home for the art of the late 19th century and the conversion of the station into a museum was entrusted to a group of youthful architects – Renaud Bardon, Pierre Colboc and Jean-Paul Philippon – assisted and coordinated by Gae Aulenti. Every time a museum is set up the foundations for a new vision of history are laid, in a cultural undertaking of profound educational and social value.

When that museum is to be located on existing premises the cultural responsibility is even greater and heaps, as it were, challenge on challenge. The totally opposite functions of a museum and a station (with the need, in the museum, to create a contemplative atmosphere and the presence, in the station, of a succession of empty and open spaces) did not discourage the architects, who succeeded in respecting and making the most of the content (the works of art) as well as the container (the preexisting architecture), both emblematic of the same Belle Époque. The conflict between conservation and change has been elegantly resolved: the challenge posed by the station stimulated their imagination, resulting in a richer and more fascinating architecture than that of a purpose-built museum. The works of art finally made their entrance in 1986: a location was found for Carpeaux's sculptures of the *Dance and the Four Quarters of the World*, while

Couture's *The Romans of the Decadence* and Courbet's picture of the people of his home town gathered for a *Burial at Ornans* were freed from their packing and, looking as if they had emerged from manuals of ancient and contemporary history, hung on the walls.

▲ **Jean-Baptiste Carpeaux,**
The Dance, 1869.

◄ **Gustave Courbet,**
Burial at Ornans, 1849.

The Collections

Painting

CLAUDE MONET,
*The Houses of Parliament.
London, Sun Breaking
Through the Fog.*

■ Continuity and revolution are the two principles that guided the artistic movements of the latter part of the 19th century: on the one hand continuity with the tradition of the great masters, fixed in precise academic rules and glorified in the Parisian exhibitions known as the Salons, and on the other a tendency toward a freer style of painting, unrestrained by such conventions. The layout of the Orsay Museum is chronological and designed to place the works in their context, revealing the close links between the various arts: sculpture, painting, decorative arts and furnishing. It begins with the pupils of Ingres and Delacroix and the great realist pictures of Courbet: onto these roots were grafted the painting of Manet and Degas and the impressionist revolution of Monet, Renoir, Pissarro and Sisley. Finally comes postimpressionism, in the different slants given to it by Cézanne, Van Gogh, Toulouse-Lautrec, Redon, Seurat, Gauguin and the Nabis movement.

Sculpture and Architecture

AUGUSTE RODIN,
Balzac, 1897.

■ The critic and writer Théophile Gautier (1811-72) asserted that "all sculpture is necessarily classical," but sculptors of great fame like Jean-Baptiste Carpeaux and Auguste Rodin show that the profile of this art was far more complex as it moved from classicism to romanticism and realism. In the second half of the 19th century, eclecticism grafted Oriental and exotic influences onto an academic base, along with a fondness for splendor and for varied, often polychrome materials. There were revolutionary trends in sculpture too, culminating in Aristide Maillol, whose works with their compact and essential forms represent both a synthesis and a surmounting of Rodin's lesson. Outstanding features of the section on architecture are the room devoted to the Opéra Garnier, reflecting the eclecticism that prevailed in the late 19th century, and drawings and plans representing the "architecture of the engineers," who used innovative materials like glass and iron.

Decorative Arts, Pastels and Drawings

EDGAR DEGAS,
The Tub, 1886.

■ The gap that had opened up in the decorative arts between aesthetic elements and functional requirements was bridged in the second half of the 19th century through a new collaboration between art and industry, celebrated at the Universal Exhibitions. Despite the spread of mass production, the elite retained their fondness for the one-off piece, like the ones made, in the fields of goldsmithry or interior decoration, by masters of the caliber of Louis C. Tiffany and Toulouse-Lautrec. The pieces on display in the museum clearly reflect the international character of the art nouveau movement, which laid the foundations of modern design, with its diverse currents in France, Scotland, Germany and Austria. The museum's collection of pastels and drawings is also of remarkable quality.

Photography

JULIA MARGARET CAMERON,
Maud, c. 1870.

■ The Musée d'Orsay was the first museum in Europe to put photographs on display, in their twofold role as works of art and historical documents. The collection, commenced in 1979, now comprises over 45 000 specimens, many of them dating from the "primitive" phase of the history of photography (from 1839 to the 1860s), during which time it was closely connected with painting and adopted its schemes, especially in portraiture (Nadar) and in the scenes of a lyrical atmosphere typical of the British school (Julia M. Cameron). Also well represented is the pictorialist movement centering on *Camera Work* (Alfred Stieglitz, Edward Steichen, Clarence White), which at the beginning of the 20th century aspired to make photography a genuine art again, a status that it had lost with the introduction of industrial production.

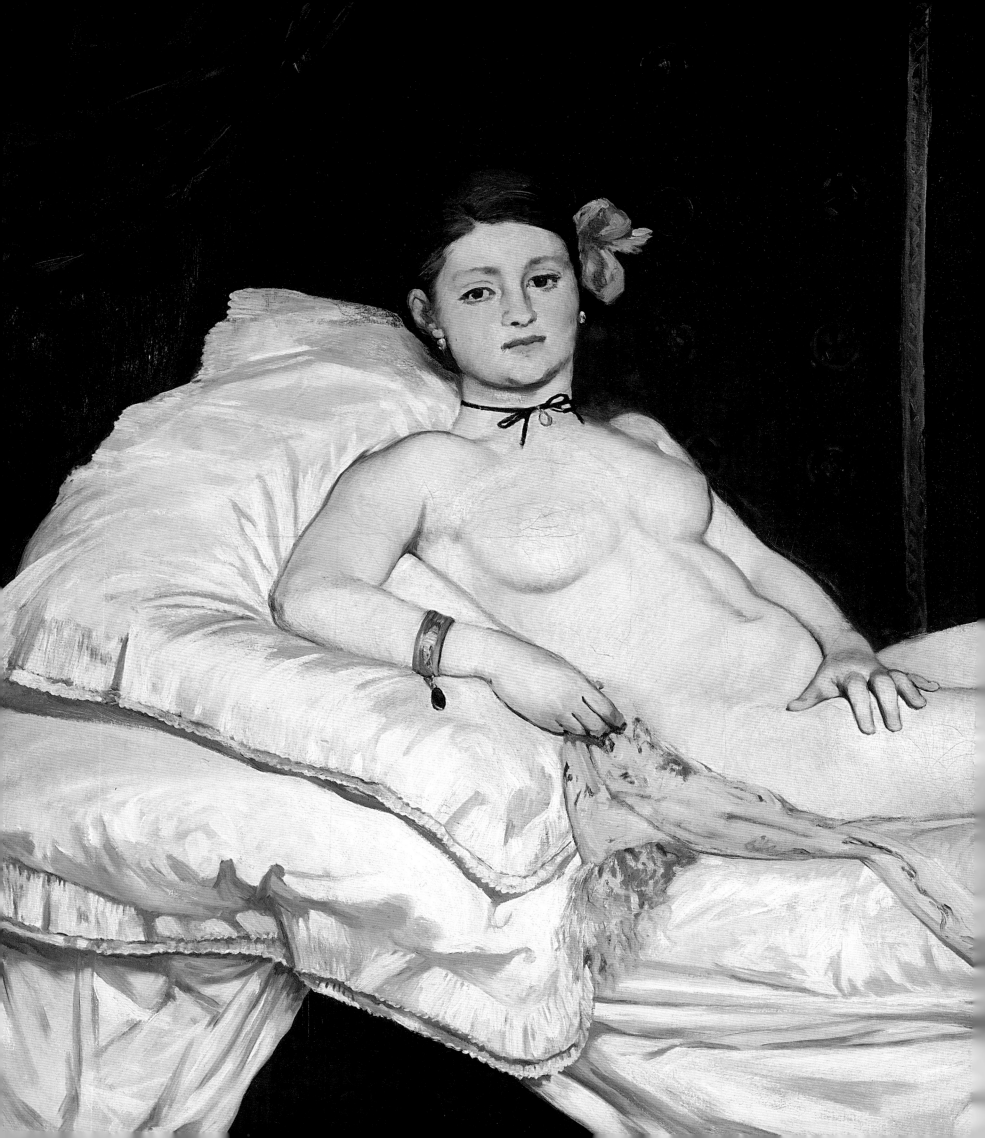

The Masterpieces

Jean-Auguste-Dominique Ingres
(1780 - 1867)

The Source

oil on canvas
64.2 x 31.5 in / 163 × 80 cm
1820 - 1856

The critic Théophile Gautier described this work as "pure Paros marble tinged with the rosy tint of life." Begun in 1820 in Florence, where the painter spent four years studying the works of the "primitives" of the 13th and 14th century and the masterpieces of the Renaissance, *The Source* was not finished until 1856. First presented in the painter's studio to a small and select group of connoisseurs, it quickly won the enthusiastic approval of both the public at large and the critics, inspiring writers and poets. As time went by its popularity only grew and the painting is still considered an authentic icon today, even if some of its edge may have been taken off by repeated reproductions. The undulating lines and soft flesh tones of the figure, much appreciated by his contemporaries, are the outcome of an intense reflection on the works of the Italian Renaissance, and in particular Ingres's favorite artist Raphael, of whom he almost considered himself a 19th century reincarnation. Unanimously regarded as the highest achievement of Ingres's classicism, *The Source* makes it easy to grasp the essence of the divide between his approach and the romantic painting of Eugène Delacroix. For their contemporaries, in fact, the two artists embodied the contrast between classicism and romanticism, between the order of a style in which drawing dominates and the freedom of one where color holds sway. Training his own pupils in the tradition of Raphael, Ingres never tired of stressing the superiority of line over color. For him a painting was nothing but a colored drawing: it is clear that he could not appreciate Delacroix's compositions, in which the objects had no sharp outlines. Many of the paintings of Ingres and Delacroix, both born at the end of the 18th century, can be seen at the Louvre, while they are represented at the Musée d'Orsay by just a few late works and by pictures painted by pupils or followers whose subject, form, style or color were influenced directly by the two artists.

◄ **Jean-Auguste-Dominique Ingres,** *La Grande Odalisque*, 1814. Musée du Louvre, Paris.

Ingres painted several pictures of Venus or of odalisques with a great feeling for the female nude, modulated by lines as elegant as arabesques and with solutions that were often highly original, breaking the traditional rules of

anatomy but perfectly convincing.

An example of this is the *Grande Odalisque*, whose complicated and contorted pose reflects an arbitrary anatomical structure, a body that seems to lack bones and muscles but is of great fascination in the musical elegance of its outlines.

The spring embodied here is represented in the classical pose of a *Venus Anadyomene* (i.e. "rising from the waters"), a pivotal theme in the history of art from antiquity to our own day.

◄ **Sandro Botticelli,** *Birth of Venus*, c. 1484. Galleria degli Uffizi, Florence.

The pictorial model is obviously Botticelli's *Birth of Venus*, which Ingres saw in Florence while he was working on the canvas. The mythological theme gave many artists the opportunity to try their hand at the female nude, taking their inspiration from Greco-Roman images of Venus or painting directly from life.

The woman's smooth and golden complexion lends warmth to a body that otherwise looks almost like a statue. Like many other elements of Ingres's art, this limpidity of the flesh tones would be widely imitated by 19th-century painters, who sought to reproduce the precious and brilliant representation of the Ancient World achieved by the master. His followers would

depict an antiquity that was cold but sensual, made up of gleaming nudes and meticulously reconstructed details. A typical example of this gelid formal perfection, reinterpreting Ingres's lesson with academic precision, is William-Adolphe Bouguereau's *Birth of Venus*, shown at the Salon in 1879.

▶ **William-Adolphe Bouguereau,** *Birth of Venus*, 1879. Musée d'Orsay, Paris.

GUSTAVE COURBET
(1819 - 1877)

Burial at Ornans

oil on canvas
124 x 263 in / 315 × 668 cm
1849 - 1850

Horrified by the painting Courbet presented to the Salon in 1851, Comte de Nieuwerkerke, the Imperial Superintendent of Fine Arts, declared: "This is the painting of democrats, of men who don't change their underwear, who want to lay down the law to polite society: art that I do not like, indeed it disgusts me." And one of the academic critics, who lost no opportunity to heap insults on Courbet's painting and the realism of which he made himself the standard-bearer, causing a scandal with every work he exhibited, wrote: "Think twice before having yourself buried at Ornans!" The critics and the jury of the Salon were closely connected with the most conservative institution of the time, the Académie de Beaux-Arts, which held despotic sway over artistic matters in France. They were the arbiters and at the same time the mouthpiece of the taste of the public, accustomed to paintings that depicted episodes from history or mythology and absolutely unprepared for the brutality of a picture like this. Courbet, refusing to make any concessions to the tastes of the public and critics, had put forward a revolutionary plan: "To be able to translate the customs, ideas and appearance of my times as I see them – in a word, to create a living art – this has been my aim."

The themes of death and the graveyard had been favorites of the romantic painters, but here the monumental dimensions of the painting elevate the representation of a funeral, an event drawn from everyday reality, to the rank of a "history painting." A history painting that does not relate something which took place in the past or the legendary exploit of a god or hero, but depicts the ordinary protagonists of the provincial life.

Monumental in scale
and with characteristics of a sculpture, the canvas becomes a sort of bourgeois historical frieze, in which the pitilessly realistic details are inserted in a studied and complex composition, made up of three homogeneous groups of figures: on the left the clergy, on the right the mourning women, in the middle the people of most importance.
All are squeezed into an almost shrunken space, flattened by the dominant tones of black.

The visitor to the
Salon, used to depictions of ancient history, or of gods, nymphs and fauns, was taken aback by the truthfulness of the representation, and especially of the figures, Courbet's fellow villagers, portrayed life size and with absolute realism. Eager to appear in the picture painted by the local artist, the inhabitants of Ornans took turns posing for Courbet, who had set up his studio in the barn of the house he had inherited from his grandfather.

Eugène Delacroix, visiting the Salon of 1850, was greatly struck by the painting. While deploring the vulgarity of the figures, he admired the prelates, the altar boys, the pot of holy water and the weeping women.

Gustave Courbet
(1819 - 1877)

The Artist's Studio

oil on canvas
141.3 x 235.4 in / 359 × 598 cm
1855

In an attempt to get his work shown at the World Exposition of 1855, Courbet painted *The Artist's Studio*, submitting it for selection along with the *Burial at Ornans*. But both pictures were rejected by the jury which, disconcerted by the strong emphasis on the material quality of the paint and the blunt representation of reality proposed by the artist, declared that "a trend in painting disastrous for French art must be checked at any cost." So Courbet decided to have an exhibition space called the Pavillon du Réalisme constructed at his own expense next to the official building, where he presented around forty works, including the two that had been rejected. But his courageous and provocative gesture did not at once meet with much success. When the painter Eugène Delacroix went to see the two controversial pictures, which he recognized as masterpieces, he spent an hour in the pavilion completely by himself, despite the considerable reduction in the entrance charge. From the complete title of the painting, *L'Atelier du Peintre, allégorie réelle, déterminant une phase de sept années de ma vie artistique* (*The Artist's Studio, a Real Allegory Determining a Phase of Seven Years of My Artistic Life*), we can deduce its programmatic intent, its character of a manifesto. In the work the painter recapitulates, through the depiction of typical representatives of social classes and actual people who had had an influence on his life since 1848, all his principles, revealing his feelings as a man and his tastes as an artist. This is why he inserted in the picture portraits of some of his friends, including Charles Baudelaire, Jules Champfleury, Pierre-Joseph Proudhon and the collector Alfred Bruyas of Montpellier. At the same time the canvases that can be seen in the studio represent the various subjects of his painting: the landscape, the female figure, portraiture, the still life and pictures of animals and the humble people he came across in the "human comedy" of real life.

The writer and
journalist Jules
Champfleury (1821-
89) is portrayed among
Courbet's friends, seated
on a bench behind the
painter. He was one of
the first critics to give his
backing to Courbet and
to his battle on behalf
of realism and would go
on to support Édouard
Manet. However, his
friendship with Courbet
was to founder after the
publication, in 1860, of
his short novel *Les amis
de la nature*, in which
Champfleury amiably
made fun of all the poets
and painters, those
"friends of nature," who
spent their days and
nights in the smoke-filled
Brasserie des Martyrs,
discussing artistic matters.

In the 1850s the poet
Charles Baudelaire,
portrayed here on the far
right, absorbed in reading,
was a friend of Courbet's,
although he was closer
to Delacroix and to the
members of the younger
generation of painters like
Manet and Fantin-Latour.
He took part in the
contemporary artistic
debate, expressing a
decided impatience with
academicism, which he
thought deprived any
artistic expression of
spontaneity.

▼ **GUSTAVE COURBET,** *Pierre-
Joseph Proudhon et ses
enfants*, 1853. Musée des
Beaux-Arts, Besançon.

The man with the beard
portrayed from the front
in the background on the
right of the painting is
the socialist philosopher
Pierre-Joseph Proudhon
(1809-65), from whom
Courbet derived many
of his theories on the
representation of the
most humble reality and
its social significance. He
guided – some would say
indoctrinated – the artist
(who painted a portrait
of him with his children),
persuading him to regard
his pictures as sociological
commentaries and to see
his work as a political tool.

JEAN-FRANÇOIS MILLET
(1814 - 1875)

The Angelus

oil on canvas
21.7 x 26 in / 55 × 66 cm
1858 - 1859

The figure of the peasant seems to have been the true protagonist of the art of the second half of the 19th century. There is nothing surprising about this if we remember that the period saw the migration of much of the population of the countryside to the urban centers, which were undergoing rapid industrial expansion. The nostalgia for the rural world that was a consequence of this phenomenon of urbanization was reflected in painting, in somewhat idealized form, through depiction of life in the fields and its eternal rhythms, associated with simple and positive values. It is significant that the first major work of art acquired by the collector Alfred Chauchard, in 1890, was Millet's *The Angelus*, coldly received by the public and critics when first shown but by now, at the end of the century, much sought after by American connoisseurs. In 1885 Alfred Chauchard had begun to assemble a collection of 19th-century French art, focusing chiefly on Millet and the landscapists of the Barbizon School (Rousseau, Corot, Daubigny...). His collection was bequeathed to the Louvre in 1909, and from there would be transferred to the Musée d'Orsay. It is said that the immediate reactions of the critics to Millet's pictures, in which humble farmers engaged in their daily labors were given the leading role, had been unanimously negative. Paul de Saint-Victor, one of the best-known writers of art of the time, wrote: "We prefer the sacred grove where fauns make their way, to the forest in which woodcutters are working; the Greek spring in which nymphs are bathing to the Flemish pond in which ducks are paddling." Thus Millet's work, which reflected a particular affection for rural life, was totally incomprehensible to the public at that time, accustomed as they were to pictures of heroic deeds or mythological events. Later the fortunes of the painting were to change, as we have seen: *The Angelus* would enjoy an extraordinary popularity and, reproduced in innumerable prints, become a sort of icon of popular piety.

The figures of the two peasants absorbed in their daily devotion are presented as static and heavy forms, almost planted in the ground that is their source of life and that feeds them from the roots. It surrounds them like a sea, extending all the way to the horizon, where we glimpse, silhouetted against the orange light of the sunset, the spire of a church. Bathed in reddish tones by the setting sun, the two figures are given a monumental character by the vigorous drawing and the simplified rendering of the forms.

Millet has often been inaccurately defined as a realist and compared with Courbet: but the only thing the two artists actually have in common is the choice of ordinary people as the subjects of their works. Millet's paintings do not limit themselves to the candid and brutal observation of reality, but in some ways transcend it, imbuing it with symbolic values: the sculptural figures of the peasants in *The Angelus*, like the famous ones of *The Gleaners*, have the solemnity of ancient bas-reliefs and their slow gestures, which convey a sense of superhuman dignity, seem to be those of a sacred rite. In *The Gleaners*, the clothes of rough fabric are depicted in dull tones, interspersed here and there by shades of pink and blue, which together with the white of a blouse form the colors of the French flag: in this way the women stooped in their hard labor, like the two peasants praying at sunset in a field, are turned into the ideal pillars, bearers of religious and moral values, on which an entire nation stands.

▲ **JEAN-FRANÇOIS MILLET,** *The Gleaners*, 1857. Musée d'Orsay, Paris.

▶ **GUSTAVE COURBET,** *Burial at Ornans*, 1849. Musée d'Orsay, Paris.

Edgar Degas
(1834 - 1917)

The Bellelli Family

oil on canvas
78.7 x 98.4 in / 200 × 250 cm
1858 - 1860

In the summer of 1858 the young Edgar Degas, in Florence on a visit to his uncle Gennaro Bellelli, with whom he had only distant relations, waited impatiently for the arrival of his aunt Laure and his two cousins, detained in Naples by the death of his grandfather Hilaire de Gas. He spent the time visiting galleries and monuments, accumulating a remarkable store of knowledge, especially of works from the early Renaissance.

In November, after his aunt and cousins came home, he enthusiastically set about painting their portrait, not to leave them a souvenir of his visit but with the aim of creating a picture that he would be able to exhibit at the Salon on his return to Paris: in fact the final dimensions of the work, probably submitted to the Salon in 1867, are the traditional ones of the history painting. Conceived in Florence and modified several times in its layout, the group portrait of the Bellelli family, completed in Paris from the numerous preparatory drawings and sketches he had made from life, is undoubtedly the masterpiece of Degas's youth.

This is evident not only from the authoritative models on which he drew (from Holbein to van Dyck) and the monumental scale of the painting, but also and above all from the carefully studied composition and the sensitive and penetrating psychological insight. Some have seen the work as a representation of the various stages of life, in that it includes not just the generations of the parents and their daughters but also, though indirectly, the as yet unborn – his aunt Laure is visibly pregnant – and the deceased – his grandfather Hilaire de Gas, whose portrait in sanguine is hanging on the wall behind, covered with flowered wallpaper. For about twenty years the painting would remain, almost unseen, in Degas's studio; suddenly brought to the attention of the public on the artist's death, it was acquired by the State at a very high price.

The extremely accurate execution of the painting is undoubtedly a product of the influence of Ingres – see for example his drawing of *The Stamaty Family* – from whom Degas took above all the precision of his line. Degas always regarded him as his ideal master, although this did not prevent him from introducing gestures or attitudes into his pictures of which Ingres would not have approved at all, giving his painting a very personal slant.

◄ **JEAN-AUGUSTE-DOMINIQUE INGRES,** *The Stamaty Family*, 1818. Musée du Louvre, Paris.

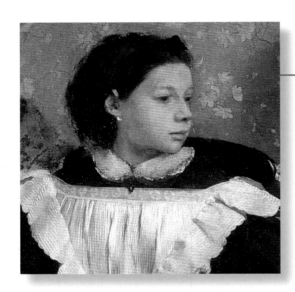

The family is rent by the lack of communication between the parents: the painter's young cousin, Giulia, with one leg folded and hidden under her skirt, is the only link between the left and right sides of the picture, between the so distant father and mother.

The artist's uncle Gennaro, who, to use the harsh words of his wife, was a man "without a steady job that would make him less boring in the family home," is portrayed from behind, on the right; concealed behind his aunt's stiff pose and haughty expression is the sadness of a troubled marriage. She had a close relationship with her painter nephew, to whom she repeatedly confided by letter her unhappiness at living in a "detestable country," alongside a husband "with an immensely unpleasant and dishonest character."

Edgar Degas
(1854 - 1917)

Semiramis Founding Babylon

oil on canvas
59.4 x 101.6 in / 151 × 258 cm
1861

In the summer of 1858, on his way to visit his aunt and uncle in Florence, Degas visited Viterbo, Orvieto, Perugia, Assisi and Arezzo. He showed a total lack of interest in the Italian landscape ("I am rapidly overcome by boredom when observing nature") and spent the whole of his time copying frescoes by Italian painters of the 14th and 15th centuries, the so-called "primitives." As far back as 1853 he had obtained permission to copy paintings at the Louvre and it was there, in contact with the old masters, that he received his real training as an artist.

By 1860 he had already made over 700 copies of works dating from the early Italian Renaissance or the French classical period and built up a stock of forms on which he was to draw repeatedly over the course of his life. And they also provided the inspiration for the unfinished painting *Semiramis Founding Babylon*, which had a long and troubled gestation and presents considerable difficulties in interpretation. On the occasion of the picture's entry into the Louvre, the critic André Michel wrote enthusiastically: "There is not one piece, not a single element of the picture – quality of the rich tones which are, at the same time, so masterly and complementary, and so delicately harmonious, grave and almost solemn simplicity of the drawing, original grouping of the figures – that does not impose itself on the mind with a slow and persuasive authority." Unfortunately this was almost the only voice raised in favor of the *Semiramis*, which was regarded by the majority, owing to its extreme complexity and unfinished state, as a failure, as a mark of Degas's inability to execute a history painting. In reality it is precisely the incompleteness of the image that makes the picture stand out from the conventional academic portrayal of historical or mythological scenes, conjuring up a world of dream: the solemnity of the figures, the frieze-like composition, the at once peaceful and heroic atmosphere and the architecture of legend give the scene a timeless ambience.

◄ **PIERO DELLA FRANCESCA**,
*The Legend of the True Cross:
The Queen of Sheba Adoring
the Cross*, 1452-62.
San Francesco, Arezzo.

The influence of Italian
models is extensive: the
most obvious is apparent
from a comparison with
one of the scenes of Piero
della Francesca's cycle in
Arezzo, *The Queen of
Sheba Adoring the Cross*.

The citation is not exact,
but from the fresco he
saw in Arezzo the painter
took the overall rhythm
of the composition
and the hieratic
character of the figures,
depicted in profile and
arranged in two main
groups: modernity and
reinterpreted tradition are
inseparably interwoven
in Degas's work.

Semiramis,
accompanied by an
entourage of handmaids,
scrutinizes from a terrace
the progress of the
construction of the city of
Babylon, which she had
founded on the banks
of the Euphrates. While
the subject is easy to
grasp, the sources from
which the painter may
have drawn inspiration
are harder to identify. In
all likelihood he got the
idea for the picture from
a performance of Rossini's
Semiramide at the Paris
Opéra in the July of 1860.

That production may have provided the inspiration, but the austere and simplified image created by Degas is very different from the Babylonian scenery used at the Opéra and draws, if anything, on a variety of archeological sources, often unidentifiable, fused together in the work in masterly fashion. As is evident from the haziness of the image, Degas, unlike in contemporary academic history painting, does not propose a meticulous reconstruction of a setting somewhere between the ancient and the exotic, but creates an original scene, remote from the mechanical citation of traditional models.

ALEXANDRE CABANEL
(1823 - 1889)

Birth of Venus

oil on canvas
51.2 x 88.6 in / 130 × 225 cm
1863

The 1863 Salon has gone down in the history of art more for the stir over its exclusions than for the works accepted for the official exhibition. Showing his paintings at the Salon, getting them a prominent position on the walls and obtaining favorable reviews in the press were the first steps toward an artist's success: the public considered the decisions of the jury final and so the artist's chances of selling his pictures and receiving new commissions were to a large extent dependent on them. In 1863 the panel of judges was particularly severe, rejecting a total of four thousand works and arousing the indignation of the painters excluded. The consequent decision of Emperor Napoleon III to stage another exhibition (known as the "Salon des Refusés") to show the works of the "rejected" artists – who included Manet, Fantin-Latour and Whistler – attracted a great deal of attention from the public, although they were more intrigued and amused by the scandal than really capable of appreciating the paintings of the young revolutionaries:

the press even went so far as to publish gossip about painters admitted to the Salon who hoped to be rejected next time in order to attract greater interest.

Leaving aside wisecracks of this kind, the work that went down best with much of the public and the critics was in reality Alexandre Cabanel's *Birth of Venus*, shown at the official Salon.

Today it is hard for us to understand why this work, with its distinctly erotic overtones, did not cause the same scandal as Édouard Manet's *Le Déjeuner sur l'herbe* presented at the Salon des Refusés. But Cabanel's painting, traditional in its formulation, concealed its real subject, a nude woman, behind the screen of myth, without dressing it up in a modern guise, and thus avoided scandalizing bourgeois morality. In fact the critics considered the picture "in no way indecent" and it fascinated all the visitors to the Salon (including the emperor, who bought it immediately), earning its author the Legion d'Honneur and election to the Académie des Beaux-Arts.

The precedents for female nudes represented in the guise of Venus were innumerable, from antiquity to Botticelli, from Giorgione and Titian to Boucher, all then all the way up to Ingres and the 19th century. Myth, like exoticism, allowed artists to paint nudes without offending morality, by projecting them far away in time and space. Exoticism provided the art of the 19th century with new subjects when it ran out of Venuses: Ingres's *Odalisque with a Slave* is a good example.

▲ **JEAN-AUGUSTE-DOMINIQUE INGRES,** *Odalisque with a Slave*, 1842. Walters Art Gallery, Baltimore.

▲ **TITIAN,** *Venus of Urbino*, 1538. Galleria degli Uffizi, Florence.

▼ **JEAN-AUGUSTE-DOMINIQUE INGRES,** *Academic Study of a Male Torso*, 1801. National Museum, Warsaw.

▼ **LAURENT PÉCHEUX,** *Pygmalion and Galatea*, 1784. Hermitage Museum, St. Petersburg.

Cabanel exemplifies the prevailing taste among the French middle class of the Second Empire: he is a typical representative of the 19th-century academic school, based on the traditional study of antiquity and the nude. Studies of the nude, whether male or female, like Ingres's *Male Torso*, were called "academic" precisely because of their "educational" character. The close relationship between the artist and his model, as in the myth of Pygmalion illustrated here by the academic painter Laurent Pécheux, was also explored by many 19th-century writers.

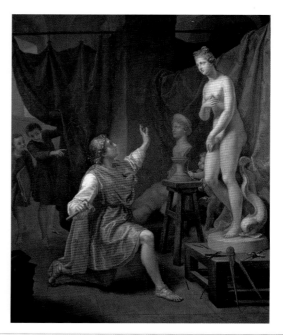

Édouard Manet
(1832 - 1883)

Le Déjeuner sur l'herbe
(The Luncheon on the Grass)

oil on canvas
81.9 x 104.1 in / 208 × 264.5 cm
1863

When *Le Bain* (*The Bath*, later renamed *Le Déjeuner sur l'herbe*, *The Luncheon on the Grass*) was shown at the Salon des Refusés in 1863, organized at the behest of Emperor Napoleon III in parallel to the official Salon as a showcase for the numerous artists who had complained at being excluded that year, the picture caused a scandal and was condemned by the public and critics alike. Curious visitors thronged around the painting, nudging each other as if they were looking at a dirty picture and taking great delight in mocking every detail of the scene represented. Émile Zola described these reactions in his novel *L'œuvre* (*The Masterpiece*): "Rumors of this picture, which was so very, very funny, must have been spreading, for there was a rush from the four corners of the Salon, bands of people arrived, jostling each other, and all eagerness to share the fun. 'Where is it?' 'Over there.' 'Oh, what a joke!' And the witticisms fell thicker than elsewhere. It was especially the subject that caused

merriment; people failed to understand it, thought it insane, comical enough to make one ill with laughter. 'You see the lady feels too hot, while the gentleman has put on his velveteen jacket for fear of catching cold.' 'Not at all; she is already blue; the gentleman has pulled her out of a pond, and he is resting at a distance, holding his nose' ." The emperor himself had branded the painting "an offense against decency," falling in line with the reviews, which had unanimously declared it indecent. What most scandalized the public and critics was the matter-of-fact realism in the depiction of the female nude in the foreground, very different from the idealized nude of the academic tradition. Although, as the painter himself revealed, the work had been inspired by Venetian models and Renaissance prints, these had done no more than provide the idea for the composition, and for the rest he had adopted a modern and unconventional language.

Perhaps Manet's picture would not have attracted so much criticism if it were not for its violent contrasts and clashes of color, in combination with a terse style of painting which did not linger over the tiniest details, as was the practice among academic painters. The "vulgarity" of which the artist was accused, therefore, stemmed not just from the subject – a woman in flesh and blood seated alongside two men in modern dress – but also from its execution.

With his perfunctory indication of the details in the background and his depiction of forms without the help of the line, simply by juxtaposing contrasting colors and sketching the outlines with a few firm strokes of the brush, Manet had adopted an extremely free style of painting that broke many of the established academic rules.

In his rendering of the woman's flesh tones Manet had abandoned the traditional precise and dense brushwork, of the kind used by Alexandre Cabanel, for example, in his *Birth of Venus*, which was accepted by the Salon of that year and won unanimous approval.

Manet himself declared that his inspiration had come from the *Country Concert*, attributed at the time to Giorgione and now to Titian, and a contemporary critic, M. Hamerton, described it in the following words: "I ought not to omit a remarkable picture of the Realist school, a translation of a thought of Giorgione into modern French. Giorgione had conceived the happy idea of a *fête champêtre* in which, although the gentlemen were dressed, the ladies were not, but the doubtful morality of the picture is pardoned for the sake of the fine color [...]. Now some wretched Frenchman has translated this into modern French realism, on a much larger scale, and with the horrible, modern French costume instead of the graceful Venetian one. Yes, there they are, under the trees, the principal lady entirely undressed [...] another female in a chemise coming out of a little stream that runs hard by, and two Frenchmen in wide-awakes [broad-brimmed hats] sitting on the very green grass with a stupid look of bliss. There are other pictures of the same class, which lead to the inference that the nude, whenever painted by vulgar men, is inevitably indecent."

ÉDOUARD MANET
(1832 - 1883)

Olympia

oil on canvas
51.4 x 74.8 in / 130.5 × 190 cm
1863

In 1865, and solely at the prompting of his friend Charles Baudelaire, Manet decided to show his *Olympia*, painted two years earlier, at the Salon. It was a spectacular flop and Baudelaire had to console the painter, demoralized by the scandal that all of his works seemed fated to cause, without him having any desire to be provocative. In fact Manet always vigorously denied that he wanted to be a revolutionary, but it is indisputable that, while finding his inspiration in the great coloristic tradition of Giorgione and Titian and in Spanish painting from Velázquez to Goya, he gave it a modern twist which inevitably scandalized his more conventional contemporaries. Manet's disillusionment and his decision to leave Paris for a while appear wholly understandable if we read the reviews of the 1865 Salon, of one mind in their moralistic condemnation of *Olympia*. The writer on art Jules Claretie spoke of "regaling the public with deceptions, send-ups, parodies and what not, yes, real travesties.

What is this Odalisque with a yellow stomach, a base model picked up I know not where, who represents Olympia?" The painting entered the collections of the Louvre (from where it later passed to the Musée d'Orsay) in 1890, as the result of an initiative on the part of Claude Monet and some of the painter's other friends, who launched a fundraising campaign to acquire for France a work they regarded as an unsurpassable example of modernity. Owing to a lengthy and heated debate, however, Manet's picture was not put on public display until 1907, when the scandal caused by his painting was subsiding. In *À la recherche du temps perdu* (*Remembrance of Things Past*), Marcel Proust has Princess Oriane de Guermantes go to see the painting shortly after it was put on show: "But really, the other day I was with the Grand Duchess in the Louvre and we happened to pass before Manet's Olympia. Nowadays nobody is in the least surprised by it. It looks just like an Ingres!"

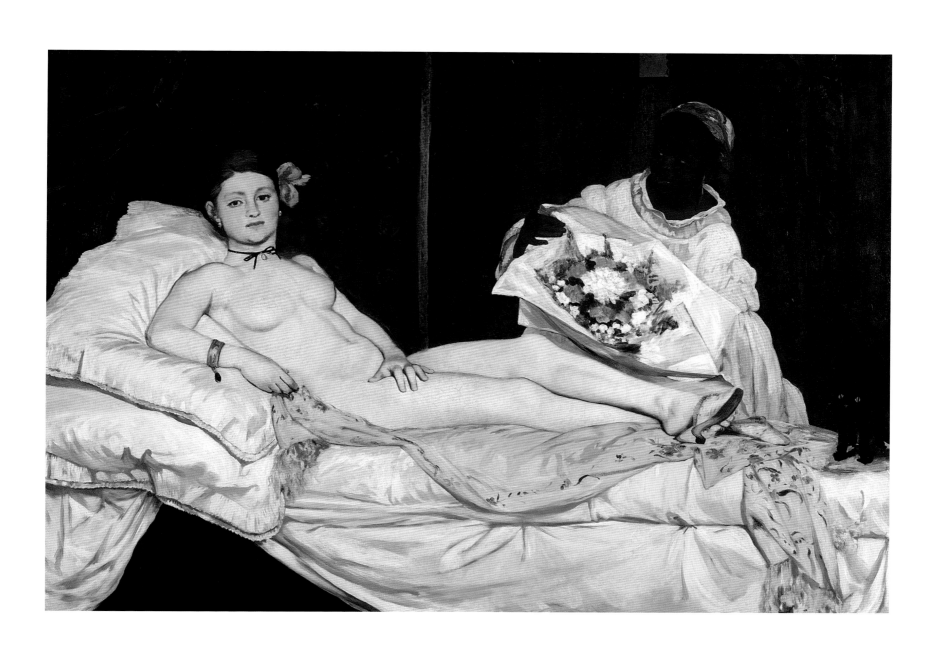

The reasons for the
scandal provoked
by the work are once
again to be sought in the
extreme freedom with
which Manet tackled
a subject codified by
tradition, that of the
female nude, even if
the artist here is clearly
making reference to a
classic model: Titian's
Venus of Urbino, alluded
to in particular by the
maid with the bunch of
flowers and the cat at the
foot of the bed.

▲ **TITIAN,** *Venus of Urbino*,
1538. Galleria degli Uffizi,
Florence.

In fact the protagonist
of Manet's picture is a
real and not an idealized
woman, staring at us with
a provocative air: she is no
Venus or odalisque, but
a modern-day prostitute.
This is clear from her
brazen pose, several
details of ostentatious
vulgarity like the jewelry
and the slippers and
even the name Olympia,
common among high-
class prostitutes (it is, for
example, the name of the
heroine's rival in Alexandre
Dumas's *La Dame aux
camélias*).

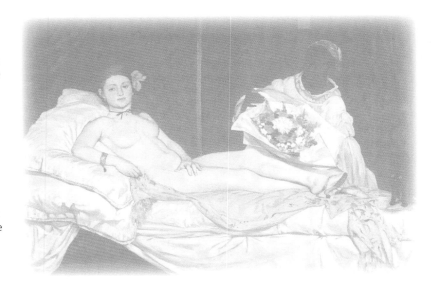

◀ **FRANCISCO GOYA,**
Maya desnuda, 1800-03.
Museo del Prado, Madrid.

The pose of the naked
woman also evokes
celebrated precedents,
such as Goya's *Maya
desnuda*, with which
Manet was undoubtedly
familiar, given the
repeated homage he paid
to Spanish painting in
every phase of his career.

From the authoritative critic Théophile Gautier came expressions of shock and concern over the phenomenon represented by Manet's realistically prosaic style of painting: "Olympia can be understood from no point of view, even if you take it for what it is, a puny model stretched out on a sheet. The color of the flesh is dirty, the modeling nonexistent. The shadows are indicated by more or less large smears of blacking. What's to be said for the negress who brings a bunch of flowers wrapped in a paper, or for the black cat which leaves its dirty footprints on the bed?"

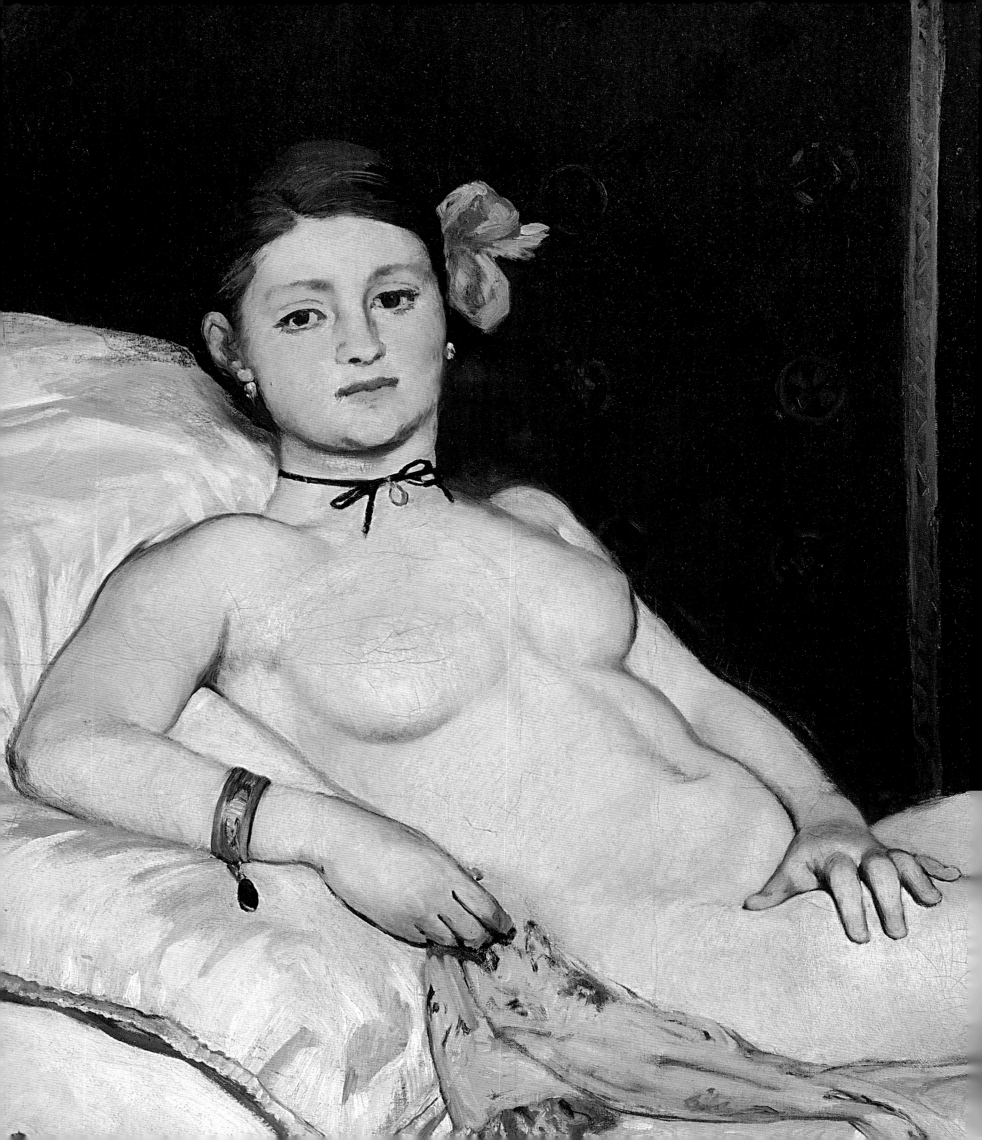

Eugène Boudin
(1824 - 1898)

The Beach at Trouville

oil on canvas
10.2 x 18.9 in / 26 × 48 cm
1864

In the 1840s Eugène Boudin had set up a stationery and picture-framing business at Le Havre to meet the needs of the numerous artists who used to spend the summer painting on the coast. In fact Honfleur, his birthplace, was the favorite haunt of many painters of seascapes, fascinated by Normandy, with its changeable skies and ever shifting light. Boudin's own activity as a painter, at first merely that of a dilettante, began to acquire importance through his contacts with artists staying on the coast: it seems that the stationer and framer's decision to devote his life to painting – and the landscape – stemmed from an encounter with Millet. In 1850 Boudin received a grant from the municipality of Le Havre that allowed him to study for three years in Paris, where he was a pupil of Isabey and Troyon, but unlike the others he did not resign himself to churning out popular genre scenes and chose instead to paint chiefly *en plein air*, soon returning to Le Havre. From Paris he brought back the conviction – repeated several times to his own pupil Claude Monet – that "the romantics have had their day. Henceforth we must seek the simple beauties of nature... nature truly seen in all its variety, its freshness."

Another fundamental event for Boudin was his meeting with Gustave Courbet in the early sixties, in the very period in which he was painting marines like this one, on the beaches at Deauville and Trouville, frequented by a crowd of elegant and frivolous middle-class people.

Getting into an argument with Courbet, who upheld the social value of his own paintings of peasants and ordinary people, he defended the subjects of his own art on the grounds of the pictorial effect of tenuous lightness conveyed by images of figures strolling on the pier at sunset. In reality Boudin was never a theorist, but remained a humble devotee of nature, to which he dedicated his own impassioned visions.

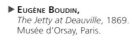

By the middle of the 19th century, the vacation at a seaside resort had taken on the character of a social ritual, in which one of the most important moments was the gathering on the beach in fashionable walking clothes. Boudin observed and transcribed these scenes in numerous sketches, drawings, pastels, watercolors and oils, which showed no hint of irony but lingered instead over the continuous play of light on the bright colors of the clothing, on the waves, on the disheveled clouds in the sky, on the loose sand.

▶ **EUGÈNE BOUDIN,** *The Jetty at Deauville*, 1869. Musée d'Orsay, Paris.

Charles Baudelaire grasped the true character of Boudin's art and, dedicating a passage filled with praise and poetic interpretations to his pastels in 1859, went so far as to claim that "only Boudin knows the sky." Baudelaire was dazzled by "these grand and beautiful skies all tormented with clouds, veiled with the most varied, deep and overpowering colors," of which he spoke with affection.

▶ **EUGÈNE BOUDIN,**
*Normandy Women Spreading
Out Washing on the Beach.*
Musée du Louvre, Paris.

Boudin is best known
today as Claude Monet's
teacher in Le Havre, the
man who encouraged
the young and talented
artist to devote himself to
landscape painting.

◀ **CLAUDE MONET,**
The Beach at Sainte-Adresse,
1867. Art Institute, Chicago.

In the sixties Monet
was a devoted pupil of
Boudin, painting side by
side with him at Le Havre
and Trouville: here we
can compare pictures
of beaches by the two
artists.

GUSTAVE MOREAU
(1826 - 1898)

Orpheus

oil on wood
60.6 x 39.2 in / 154 × 99.5 cm
1866

The myth of Orpheus, one of the favorite themes of symbolist painting as it speaks of the immortality an artist can attain through his creations, is here given one of its most original interpretations. Orpheus was a poet, the son of Apollo, whom the Muses themselves had taught to play the lyre he had been given by his father. His music and his verses were so sweet and captivating that, in order to listen to them, water slowed its flow in the streams, birds ceased to fly, nymphs emerged from their hiding places and wild beasts came out from their lairs. When his wife, the nymph Eurydice, was killed by a snakebite, the despairing Orpheus descended into the underworld, the kingdom of the dead. He so moved the god Hades with his music that Orpheus was allowed to take Eurydice with him, on condition that he did not turn round to look at her during the journey. But Orpheus could not resist and Eurydice vanished forever into the infernal depths. From that moment on he scorned the entire female sex, rousing the ire of the Maenads, the priestesses of Dionysus, who tore him to pieces and threw his remains into the Hebrus River, in Thrace.

The head remained afloat and continued to sing: "Eurydice – ah, poor Eurydice! 'Eurydice' the banks re-echoed, all along the stream." (Virgil, *Georgics*). In this painting, which received a favorable reception when it was shown at the Salon of 1866 and was immediately purchased by the State, Moreau depicts the final part of the myth, when Orpheus's head is fished out of the river by a Thracian girl, who gazes at it enchanted, in a desolate and timeless landscape. Drawn to the exoticism he had learned to appreciate from his teacher, the Orientalist painter Théodore Chassériau, Moreau adds a touch of surreal fantasy, of often sensual and murky reverie that sets him apart from his contemporaries and renders difficult any attempt to define his art, in which the symbolist style is interpreted in an eccentric way and with a taste for sumptuous decoration.

The myth of Orpheus and Eurydice has fascinated artists, poets and musicians of every age, who have largely chosen to illustrate the first part of the myth: see for example Rubens's painting of the couple leaving the Underworld. Moreau often reinterpreted myth, as well as history and stories from the Bible, from a perspective that was at once sensual and introspective. Rarely did he represent the action as it unfolded, choosing to focus instead on secondary moments: in this case one in which, after the violence of the events had abated, the young woman reflects on the art and the love of Orpheus, which had been able to overcome death.

▲ **PIETER PAUL RUBENS,** *Orpheus and Eurydice*, 1636-38. Museo del Prado, Madrid.

▼ **GUSTAVE MOREAU,** *Jason and Medea*, 1865. Musée d'Orsay, Paris.

Moreau's gifts as a painter – one might even say those of a miniaturist – and his leaning toward a sumptuous aestheticism are most apparent in the incidental details that he inserts in his compositions: note, for example, the jewelry applied on the Thracian girl's dress, or the column in his *Jason and Medea*, encrusted with pearls, cameos and multicolored gems.

During the years from which this picture dates Moreau's compositions grew increasingly complex, as he filled them with a variety of refined elements that created a climate of precious and sensual sanctity.
What stands out in this work is the rich and sophisticated brushwork, with the forms and details sometimes painstakingly defined in an academic manner (as in the girl's face), while at others the paint is laid on in a thick impasto, as in the landscape in the background.

CLAUDE MONET
(1840 - 1926)

Women in the Garden

oil on canvas
100.4 x 80.7 in / 255 × 205 cm
1866 - 1867

At the time this painting was rejected by the Salon, in 1867, Claude Monet was twenty-seven years old and filled with new ideas and enthusiasm, but his financial situation was extremely precarious. The impossibility of showing the picture at the Salon, which might have helped to establish his reputation, put the young man in a tight spot, from which he was only able to escape as a result of the purchase of the work by his friend Frédéric Bazille. It is no surprise that the painting had been rejected: the panel responsible for selection of the works for the Salon was particularly hostile to the "deplorable direction" that young artists were taking.

Only Émile Zola was able to grasp the value of the painting, defending it in a review he wrote: "They have rejected one of his pictures of figures in which several women in pale summer dresses were picking flowers on the path of a garden; the sun's rays fell straight on the dazzling white skirts; the feeble shadow of a tree spread a great gray pall over the path, over the dresses awash with sunlight [...]. One has to have a great love for one's own time to attempt such a *tour de force*." Within the group of painters who would later come to be known as

impressionists, Monet was perhaps the most faithful to its anti-academic principles, and in particular to the one that called for the artist to get out of his studio and paint nature from life. The main factors behind Monet's revolutionary choice of working *en plein air* ("in the open air") were his aversion for the official art of the Salon, his interest in realism and the landscapes of the Barbizon School and a distaste for the themes – which he found boring and insignificant – preferred by the bourgeoisie. Out of his feverish activity of painting from life in the forest of Fontainebleau came the numerous landscapes of those years and his study of figures in the open, illuminated by light filtering through the foliage of trees: one of the first products of this research was *Women in the Garden*, whose highly innovative technique of painting immediately disqualified the artist in the eyes of official criticism, leading to his rejection at the Salon.

Here Monet has worked with broad brushes and rapid touches, applying thick layers of paint in vivid colors in an attempt to "catch" the reflections of light on the summer fabrics of the dresses, on the flowers and on the leaves.

Similar in its subject to the *Women in the Garden* is *Le Déjeuner sur l'herbe* (*The Picnic*), painted by Monet the year before as a direct response to Édouard Manet's own and more famous *Déjeuner*. Monet had in mind an ambitious composition depicting a group of picnickers who would differ from Manet's figures in the natural lighting and the casual attitudes and poses of a Sunday outing. Unfortunately the artist never managed to finish the painting, which he later cut into three pieces: for an idea of what it looked like we have to rely on the study in the Pushkin Museum and the fragments in the Musée d'Orsay. Manet, much more traditional in his approach in those years, did not appear to appreciate the spontaneity of his youthful colleague's painting. It seems that on seeing one of Monet's pictures he had remarked: "But look at this young man who is trying to paint in the open air! As if such a thing had ever occurred to the ancients!" The statement shows the distance between the two artists and explains the differences between the two pictures.

▲ **CLAUDE MONET,** *Study for Le Déjeuner sur l'herbe*, 1866. Pushkin Museum, Moscow.

▲ **ÉDOUARD MANET,** *Le Déjeuner sur l'herbe*, 1863. Musée d'Orsay, Paris.

◀ **CLAUDE MONET,** *Le Déjeuner sur l'herbe*, central part, 1866. Musée d'Orsay, Paris.

Here Monet has worked with broad brushes and rapid touches, applying thick layers of paint in vivid colors in an attempt to "catch" the reflections of light on the summer fabrics of the dresses, on the flowers and on the leaves.

FRÉDÉRIC BAZILLE
(1841 - 1870)

Family Reunion

oil on canvas
59.8 x 90.6 in / 152 × 230 cm
1867

For once, in 1868, the young artists of the group centered on Édouard Manet had the pleasant surprise of having the works they submitted to the Salon accepted. That year, in fact, one of the members of the jury was Charles Daubigny, the painter whom a few years earlier they had got to know in the forest of Fontainebleau, working alongside them and experimenting with painting *en plein air*. To get the pictures of his protégés admitted, Daubigny exerted considerable pressure on the Superintendent of Fine Arts Nieuwerkerke, eventually getting his way. Among those accepted were pictures by Pissarro, Monet, Renoir, Sisley and Bazille, who had submitted his *Family Reunion*. The former were the principal exponents of the impressionist group: Bazille, who had taken part in the research it conducted until 1870, would have been too, if he had not fallen, at the age of just twenty-nine, in the Franco-Prussian War, killed at the battle of Beaune-la-Rolande.

While spending the summer of 1867 on his parents' estate, near Montpellier, Bazille began work on a large composition in which all the members of his family are portrayed on a shady terrace, including his own self-portrait on the far left. The house at Montpellier was located not far from that of Alfred Bruyas, a collector and a friend of Courbet, who still exercised an influence on the young Bazille in this period. Unlike his friends, obliged to lead a Bohemian life owing to the opposition of their families to their artistic calling, Bazille had been able to reach a compromise with his parents, who had allowed him to go to Paris and to divide his time equally between studying medicine and art.

In Paris he frequented the atelier of Charles Gleyre along with Monet, Sisley and Renoir, and on more than one occasion helped out his friends in their often precarious financial situation, allowing them to work for months at a time in his own studio.

The Family Reunion
displays an acute
sensitivity to light, which
cuts the planes sharply,
accentuating the contrasts
and the solidity of the
forms. The originality
of the layout and the
gamut of colors indicate
the importance of the
example set by the older
Manet's *Le Déjeuner sur
l'herbe*, with its clearly
outlined volumes and
rigorous drawing.

▶ **ÉDOUARD MANET,**
Le Déjeuner sur l'herbe, 1863.
Musée d'Orsay, Paris.

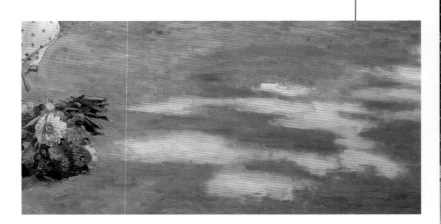

The link between
Bazille and his
contemporary Monet
is evident in the
representation of the
sunlight which, filtered
by the leaves of the trees,
casts distinct shadows
on the ground and
transforms the coloring
of the clothes: all this is
reminiscent of *Women in
the Garden*, painted by his
friend Monet that same
summer.

▶ **CLAUDE MONET,** *Women in
the Garden*, 1866-67. Musée
d'Orsay, Paris.

◀ **PIERRE-AUGUSTE RENOIR,**
Portrait of Bazille, 1867.
Musée d'Orsay, Paris.

In the fall of 1869 Bazille
rented a large studio on
Rue de la Condamine, in
the Batignolles quarter,
where his friend Renoir
also came to work and
portrayed him at the
easel.

▶ **FRÉDÉRIC BAZILLE,**
The Artist's Studio, 1870.
Musée d'Orsay, Paris.

Bazille was so fascinated
by his studio that he
decided to commemorate
it in a picture,
representing his friends
in a group portrait.
Unlike Fantin-Latour,
who always presented
his models in an almost
solemn pose, he depicted
the studio with all the
informality that usually
held sway there. While
Edmond Maître plays
the piano, Émile Zola is
on the stairs talking to
Renoir, who is sitting on
a table. Édouard Manet
is looking at a picture
on the easel. Behind him
Claude Monet, smoking,
is looking at it too, and
Bazille is standing by
them, with the palette in
his hand: after the artist
finished portraying his
friends, Manet had taken
the brushes and added
the figure of Bazille.

◀ **HENRI FANTIN-LATOUR,**
A Studio in the Batignolles,
1870. Musée d'Orsay, Paris.

Édouard Manet
(1832 - 1883)

Portrait of Émile Zola

oil on canvas
57.6 x 44.9 in / 146.3 × 114 cm
1867 - 1868

Émile Zola, caught here at a moment when, lifting his eyes from the book in his hands, he turns slightly toward the observer, was the rising star of French literature in these years: his first naturalistic novel, *Thérèse Raquin*, had come out in 1867 and he was just getting started on the twenty-volume series *Les Rougon-Macquart*. Zola was also the critical voice with a markedly polemic spirit whose incisive newspaper articles inevitably provoked scandal and heated debate: his writings on literature and art were presented as declarations of poetics, as his backing, on paper, for movements considered subversive. The meeting with Manet, the visit to his studio and the association with the artists who would later be called impressionists were extremely important for Zola, who on several occasions would defend his friends against their ostracism by the conservative critics of the Salon. His close relationship with Manet is attested by the pamphlet devoted to him by the writer, which can be seen in the portrait behind the inkwell on the small desk covered with books. In it Zola wrote: "Manet's place is marked out in the Louvre, like Courbet's, like that of every artist with a strong and unrelenting temperament." It was a prediction that came true, and the painting would later be transferred from the Louvre to the Musée d'Orsay. The painter presents us his friend in the guise of an intellectual, taken by surprise in the intimacy of his study, his expression concentrated and absorbed, like those 15th- and 16th-century portraits of men of letters in their "cabinets": a mark, this, of the attention Manet paid to the old masters, studied on his frequent visits to the Louvre. In the background, along with a Japanese print and a sketch of the *Olympia*, there is an engraving of Velázquez's *The Triumph of Bacchus*, a tribute to the great Spanish painting Manet had rediscovered on his frequent visits to that country. These works, together with the *Olympia*, which caused such a scandal at the Salon in 1865, constitute a programmatic declaration in images, a sign of mutual understanding between the artist and the observer that indicates both the sources of his painting and his own idea of modernity, based on incisive innovations in the way of applying the paint and composing the picture and on ideas derived from the tradition of the Far East.

▶ *Print with a view
of the Universal
Exposition in Paris.*

An entire Japanese farmhouse was presented at the Universal Exposition held in Paris in 1867, faithfully reproduced and furnished with articles of everyday use: the public, fascinated by the exotic atmosphere, began to collect fans and prints, lacquers and all sorts of other objects, following the example of the artists who had been indulging in this new passion for a decade already.

Both Manet and Zola were enthusiastic admirers and collectors of Japanese artifacts and prints: note, in the painting, the screen to the left of the sitter and the print of a sumo wrestler, work of the artist Kuniaki II Utagawa (1853-88). Zola, in his little book on Manet, showed that he understood the influence that his friend's knowledge of Japanese art had had on the formal and compositional innovation of his works: "he passes from black to white without hesitation, renders the various objects with vigor so that they are detached from one another. His whole being leads him to see in patches, in simple and strong fragments."

▶ **Vincent Van Gogh,**
Le père Tanguy, 1887.
Niarchos Collection, Paris.

What today might seem a curious vogue or mania – the custom that artists of the time had of collecting prints and artifacts from the Far East and reproducing them in their own paintings (as van Gogh did in his *Le père Tanguy*) and of drawing on their simplified style as a source of inspiration for the renewal of their art – was in fact a widespread phenomenon, known as Japonisme, that influenced the taste of an era not just through its effects on fashion, but also and above all for the important repercussions that it had on Western art and culture.

Jean-Baptiste Carpeaux
(1827 - 1875)

The Dance

stone
165.4 x 117.3 in / 420 × 298 cm
1869

To justify the decorative exuberance of the Opéra in Paris, which he had built in the 1860s, the architect Charles Garnier declared: "It is art that will be staying there and art should not sully itself with timidity; it is only necessary for the richness to have dignity, for art, while it can dance the gavotte and the minuet, must abstain from the cancan." Perhaps he was thinking of Jean-Baptiste Carpeaux's sculpture *The Dance*, set on the building's façade. The new Opera House is the most emblematic of the operations carried out within the framework of the urban redevelopment of Paris undertaken on the orders of Napoleon III. For fifteen years the city was an immense construction site, as Émile Zola records: "Paris gutted with blows of the sword, her open veins nourishing a hundred thousand laborers and builders." The Opéra Garnier is the most typical architectural expression of the Second Empire, characterized by an eclectic interpretation of the models of the past and a wealth of ornamentation that spurns any kind of rationality.

Along the base of the theater's sumptuous façade are set four sculptural groups, which were supposed to represent Comedy and Drama, Lyric Poetry and Light Poetry, Song and Music and Amorous Dance and Bacchic Dance. It was Garnier himself who imposed on the sculptors the common scheme of the groups, which, like all the decorative elements, had to blend in harmoniously with the architecture. But after a long period of gestation – three years of tireless research – Carpeaux, who owed the commission to his longstanding friendship with the architect, eventually produced a composition that, while it failed to meet the initial conditions, delighted Garnier nonetheless. Unveiled in 1869, the work immediately caused a scandal and the wild dance of nude figures was described as an "ignoble Saturnalia," an "insult to public morality." However, the decision to replace it with another *Dance*, executed by the sculptor Charles-Antoine-Achille Gumery, was never implemented as a result of the outbreak of the Franco-Prussian war in 1870.

Jean-Baptiste Carpeaux,
Four Quarters of the World,
1890. Musée d'Orsay, Paris.

The same circular scheme is found in one of Carpeaux's last major works, the fountain of the *Four Quarters of the World* executed for the garden of the observatory. In it Carpeaux represents the four cardinal points turning as if to follow the rotation of the Earth, so that the figures are shown simultaneously from more than one angle, from the front, at three quarters, in profile and from behind.

The sculptural group, made up of five figures encircling a male spirit who is flinging himself joyfully forward, is the most significant work of Carpeaux's maturity: drawing on an exceptional knowledge of the human body, he realized here his ideal of expressing the vibrancy of life and movement. The group is perfectly harmonious and balanced, self-contained in its rotary movement and at the same time opening up impetuously toward the observer.

Threatened by atmospheric pollution, the original group was transferred to the Louvre in 1964 and then to the entrance hall of the Musée d'Orsay. Its place has been taken by a copy made by the sculptor Paul Belmondo.

▶ *Opéra Garnier*, Paris.

Edgar Degas
(1834 - 1917)
The Orchestra of the Opéra

oil on canvas
22.2 x 18.2 in / 56.5 × 46.2 cm
1869

At the end of the 1860s Degas began to hang around the wings of the Paris Opéra, where he found new motifs and subjects for his painting. He visited the classes where the dancing master trained girls in the demanding art of ballet, sketching the contortions of their bodies in terse and clean lines.

He made friends with a musician in the orchestra, Désiré Dihau, and inserted his portrait in paintings that are among his most innovative in their composition and most daring in their layout, with the scene relegated to the background while the musicians and their instruments occupy the foreground. In this way Degas's interests started to shift toward a new conception of painting, whose aim was no longer to represent antiquity, but the day-to-day heroism of modern life, which Charles Baudelaire regarded as the principal theme of art: "He shall be the true painter who can pull out of everyday life its epic side."

And in particular: "The life of our city is rich in poetic and marvelous subjects. We are enveloped and steeped as though in an atmosphere of the marvelous; but we do not notice it." With his keen interest in the present, that is to say in modern Paris with its cafés, racecourses, theaters and *boulevards*, Degas created fleeting and immediate images that offered a cross section of the society of his time, observed and studied with extraordinary sensitivity and insight. The painting entered the Louvre (and then the Musée d'Orsay) from the collection of Désiré Dihau and his sister Marie, which included some of the most innovative of the works of Degas and Toulouse-Lautrec, lovingly selected and acquired by its owners. In 1928 Marie Dihau, although in financial difficulties, chose to spend her last years living on a pension paid to her by Toulouse-Lautrec's mother and the Louvre rather than part with her paintings.

The Orchestra of the *Opéra* was conceived as a portrait of the musician Désiré Dihau, shown here playing the bassoon. Twenty years later the young Henri de Toulouse-Lautrec was to meet the painter he regarded as his master at the home of Désiré and Marie Dihau, his cousins and enthusiastic collectors of Degas's work. After painting portraits of his cousins, Toulouse-Lautrec was able to compare his own work with Degas's every time he paid a visit. Marie Dihau, formerly a successful singer and later a piano teacher, was painted by both artists seated at the piano, in front of the score and in unconventional poses; her brother Désiré, on the other hand, was portrayed in his official role as a musician of the Opéra.

◄ **Henri de Toulouse-Lautrec,** *Mademoiselle Dihau at the Piano*, 1890. Musée Toulouse-Lautrec, Albi.

► **Edgar Degas,** *Mademoiselle Dihau*, 1869-72. Musée d'Orsay, Paris.

The highly original composition is divided horizontally into two separate parts: Dihau and the other musicians, in the foreground, are in semidarkness and the ballerinas, looking like specters in the brilliant illumination of the footlights, are cut off by the upper edge of the canvas, creating the impression of a photograph.

The low point of view gives the painting a peculiar slant, offering an unusual view of theatrical life: the protagonists of the picture are the normally invisible musicians of the orchestra, concealing the stage on which the real spectacle is taking place. The illuminated legs and skirts of the ballerinas form a strong and lively contrast of color with the group of musicians, projecting the bright light of the boards against the darkness of the hall.

Henri Fantin-Latour
(1836 - 1904)
A Studio in the Batignolles

oil on canvas
80.3 x 107.7 in / 204 × 273.5 cm
1870

At the end of the 1860s, before the outbreak of the Franco-Prussian War disrupted the vibrant cultural life of Paris and the existence of many of its protagonists, artists used to meet in the late afternoon – when the failing light obliged them to put down their brushes – at the city's cafés. At number 11, Rue de Batignolles (afterward renamed Avenue de Clichy), was located the Café Guerbois, where Édouard Manet could often be found surrounded by young artists interested in the research he was conducting. Their long discussions turned on technical and formal matters and on the recent experiments with painting *en plein air*.

Claude Monet would later recall: "Nothing could be more interesting than these causeries with their perpetual clash of opinions. They kept our wits sharpened, they encouraged us with stores of enthusiasm that for weeks and weeks kept us up until the final shaping of the idea was accomplished. From them we emerged tempered more highly, with a firmer will, with our thoughts clearer and more distinct." Although very different in character and professing different ideas, the *habitués* of the Café Guerbois, often divided and independent in their research, were united by a common desire for revolutionary change and constituted what was known as the Batignolles Group. Alongside Manet, who was its true intellectual leader (as is clear from this painting, an out-and-out homage to the artist), its most prominent members were Pissarro, Degas and Fantin-Latour. It was the latter who brought them all together in a portrait with Manet at its center, omitting for the first time to place himself among the companions, as if he realized that he was no longer part of the group. While closely linked to the impressionists, whom he admired and whose rejection of official and academic painting he shared, Henri Fantin-Latour was an independent figure, remaining faithful to his own brand of lyrical realism, couched in subdued and mellow harmonies.

Always well groomed, Manet was, according to Zola, "of medium height, more short than tall; blond haired, with a slightly red face, keen, intelligent eyes, [his] restless mouth turning ironic now and again; the whole of his expressive, irregular face has an indefinable finesse and vigor about it [...]. For the rest, he has the greatest modesty and kindness in his manners."

Fantin-Latour described the people he portrayed around Manet while he worked as follows: Renoir, in the hat, "a painter who will get himself talked about"; Zacharie Astruc, seated in the foreground, a "fantastic poet"; Émile Zola, standing next to Renoir, a "realist novelist, great defender of Manet in the newspapers"; to his right, Edmond Maître, a "sharp mind, amateur musician"; then the great Bazille, "who is a promising talent," with Claude Monet standing behind him. To the left of Manet with his eyes fixed on the canvas, the German painter Otto Scholderer.

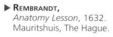 **REMBRANDT,** *Anatomy Lesson*, 1632. Mauritshuis, The Hague.

The theme of the composition is a modern reinterpretation of Rembrandt's celebrated *Anatomy Lesson*.

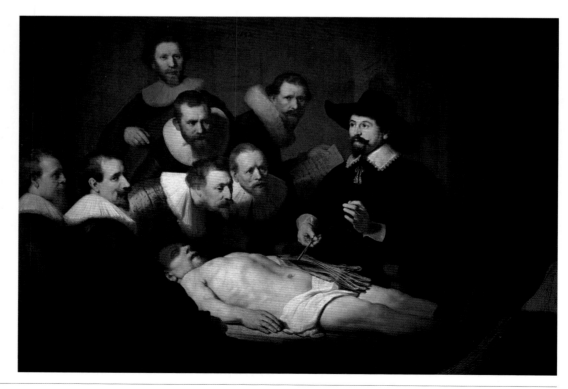

Émile Zola, a writer at the peak of his literary career, a critic whose reviews frequently appeared in the papers and a close friend of Manet, had assumed the role of defender of the artists who were to form the impressionist movement, even though he was not fully in agreement with the direction they took in their theoretical research and only appreciated the results in part.

▲ HENRI FANTIN-LATOUR, *Homage to Delacroix*, 1863. Musée d'Orsay, Paris.

The death of Delacroix, on August 13, 1863, gave Fantin-Latour the idea of painting a picture in his honor. Around a portrait of the artist, seen as the initiator of the revolt against academic art, he gathered those of his friends and acquaintances who, like him, were sincere admirers of the painter. The group comprises all Delacroix's followers and admirers since the time his first works were shown at the Salon.

Standing, from left to right: Cordier, Legros, Whistler, Manet, Bracquemond and Balleroy. Seated: Duranty, Fantin-Latour, Champfleury and Baudelaire.

The artist exhibited this ambitious composition at the Salon in 1864, even though he was not satisfied with it, considering that it had come out too dark.

JAMES ABBOTT MCNEILL WHISTLER
(1834 - 1903)

Arrangement in Gray and Black, No. 1: The Artist's Mother

oil on canvas
56.8 x 64 in / 144.3 × 162.5 cm
1871

After making his first visit to France in 1855, the American James Abbott McNeill Whistler divided his time between Paris and London, but was long excluded from the official artistic circles of both countries as a result of his provocative behavior and his skill at what he himself called the "noble art of making enemies." Whistler was one of many artists from all over the world who were drawn to Paris by the impressionist movement, absorbing its revolutionary lesson and interpreting the new style in highly personal ways. The artist painted this picture of his mother, Anna Matilda McNeill, between August and October of 1871, when she was living in his house in London. In a letter to her sister, the elderly lady confided that during the sittings for the portrait she used to pray that her son would achieve success: for years in fact Whistler was opposed by the official critics and his mother did not live long enough to see his final acceptance, marked by the retrospective held in 1892 at the Goupil gallery.

Whistler's Mother, as the picture is popularly known, gave the artist an opportunity to experiment with a formal and chromatic harmony that went beyond the representation of the subject, in keeping with his repeated claim that in painting it was not the theme that counted, but the way in which it was translated into forms and colors. Emblematic, in this sense, is the fact that the painter exhibited the work in 1872 under the title *Arrangement in Gray and Black*, without stating that it was a portrait of his mother. Criticized for this in England, as well as for the excessive severity of the composition and his failure to enrich the scene with details, Whistler's sarcastic response was to suggest that the public could be satisfied by adding a glass of sherry and placing a Bible in the woman's hands.

Whistler shared his friend Édouard Manet's enthusiasm for Japanese prints. He made the simplification of space and color typical of that tradition the foundation of his own style. In a work like *Whistler in His Studio*, in fact, the simplified lines and refined harmonies of neutral shades, the liquid and vaporous brushwork and the indifference to the rules of perspective are principally variations on the theme of Japanese prints: as in Whistler's other works, the subject represented is of little importance.

▲ **James Abbott McNeill Whistler**, *Whistler in His Studio*, 1865. Art Institute of Chicago, Chicago.

▲ **James Abbott McNeill Whistler**, *Symphony in White, No. 2: The Little White Girl*, 1864. Tate Gallery, London.

▼ **Antonio Canova**, *Portrait of Letizia Ramolino Bonaparte*, 1804. Museo di Capodimonte, Naples.

▶ *Agrippina Seated*, second half of 1st century AD. Musei Capitolini, Rome.

The austerity of the painting is derived in part from classical models of maternal portraits, images of haughty matrons presented in similar poses: for example the *Seated Agrippina*, which also served Antonio Canova as a model for his portrait of Napoleon's mother.

The painter's mother, a very devout woman, is portrayed in a pose that expresses a pious resignation to the hard trials of life (in her case, the death of her husband and two children): in her dress and attitude, the elderly lady has the appearance of a severe icon of the Protestant religion.

BERTHE MORISOT
(1841 - 1895)

The Cradle

oil on canvas
22 x 18.1 in / 56 × 46 cm
1872

Daughters of a wealthy magistrate, the sisters Berthe and Edma Morisot began to study painting in Paris in 1857: not as "wellborn" young ladies for whom drawing and painting were a genteel pastime, like embroidery or playing the piano, but with application and passion. Berthe, in particular, used to surprise visitors to the Louvre by the tenacity with which she copied the works of the great masters.

Very soon, however, the two sisters grew dissatisfied with the traditional method of training and were introduced to Corot, throwing themselves enthusiastically into painting the landscape from nature, in the manner of Corot himself and the painters of the Barbizon School. Around 1835 the latter, active in the environs of Fontainebleau, had ventured outdoors to paint in direct contact with nature, making sketches that they then reworked in the studio. The group of impressionists, of which Berthe Morisot was an enthusiastic member right from the start, were to take a further and fundamental step: that of completing the whole of a painting *en plein air*, in the immediacy of a spontaneous execution, no longer perfected "in cold blood."

The Cradle, one of the artist's best-known pictures, was shown at the first exhibition of the impressionists, held from April to May in 1874. Like all the works by members of the group presented on that occasion, it created a scandal. In particular it was the new technique, unconstrained by the academic rules of accurate drawing and precise brushwork, that aroused controversy. The critic Louis Leroy wrote, sarcastically: "Now take Mademoiselle Morisot! That young lady is not interested in reproducing trifling details. When she has a hand to paint she makes exactly as many brushstrokes lengthwise as there are fingers and the business is done. Stupid people who are finicky about the drawing of a hand don't understand a thing about impressionism, and [...] Manet would chase them out of his republic."

▲ **Berthe Morisot,**
The Butterfly Hunt, 1874.
Musée d'Orsay, Paris.

Like Renoir, Berthe Morisot was a past master at the painting of figures and scenes of family intimacy, excelling in the depiction of female coquetry and elegance, the joys of motherhood and children at play, as in *The Butterfly Hunt*. A painter of feminine charm in all its expressions, she was able to represent it with equal efficacy and freedom in the splendid and chaotic setting of the big city and in the lazily peaceful one of the countryside or the family home.

ÉDOUARD MANET,
The Balcony, 1868-69.
Musée d'Orsay, Paris.

At the Salon of 1868 Berthe Morisot met Édouard Manet and agreed to pose for him. Berthe was undoubtedly in love with the artist, but it was Manet's brother Eugène who eventually married her, in 1874.

From these sittings the painter derived the absorbed and enigmatic figure holding a fan in *The Balcony*, exhibited at the Salon of 1869, where it is possible to discern the influence of the delicate tones favored by Morisot. The following year he painted her portrait again, perched on a sofa.

▲ **ÉDOUARD MANET,** *Portrait of Berthe Morisot*, 1869. Museum of Art, Rhode Island School of Design, Providence.

▶ **BERTHE MORISOT,**
At the Ball, 1875.
Musée Marmottan, Paris.

Morisot was strongly influenced by Manet and, later on, by Claude Monet. Yet she was able to develop an original approach of her own, especially in the chromatic intensity of her works: the critic Théodore Duret commented that the artist, when completing her pictures, seemed to sprinkle them with many-colored flower petals at the last moment. A vibrant coloring that expresses a delight in creation akin to Renoir's.

Claude Monet
(1840 - 1926)

Poppies

oil on canvas
19.7 x 25.6 in / 50 × 65 cm
1873

Émile Zola described the curiosity of the public, come to amuse themselves at the first independent joint exhibition of the young impressionists, held in the studio of the photographer Félix Nadar from April 15 to May 15, 1874, as follows: "The ladies no longer stifled their laughter with their handkerchiefs, and the men distended their stomachs in order to vent theirs with greater ease [...]. They nudged one another, doubled over [...] each canvas was subjected to appraisal and people called to each other to point out a good one, witticisms passed from mouth to mouth [...]." The catalogue was edited by Edmond Renoir, the painter's brother, and Monet had driven him crazy by sending too many pictures and exasperated him with the monotony of their titles: *Entrance of a Village, Leaving the Village, Morning in a Village* and the like. When Edmond protested, Monet calmly told him: "Why don't you just put Impression." His reply revealed the scant importance of the subject in a painting that set out to capture the visual perception of nature with immediacy, i.e. the "impression." So the group accepted the definition of impressionism for their approach to painting. It was a name that the critics took up, using it in a disparaging sense as they considered the works to be uncultured and superficial. The picture, shown on this occasion along with many others by Monet, is the product of a dazzling vision, an attempt to capture the light of a sunny afternoon through color. This time it was not the presumed immorality of the subject that so upset the public and the critics, as had been the case with certain "realistic" paintings, but the completely new technique, totally unconstrained by academic rules, which laid down that color had to be subordinate to drawing. In fact the joke went round that the method used by these painters was to load a pistol with various tubes of paint and shoot them at the canvas, and then add their signature.

The painting can be compared with the *Path Through the Long Grass*, painted a year later by Pierre-Auguste Renoir, a friend of the painter since the time of their training and in those years his companion on excursions into the country, where the two painted side by side *en plein air*. The paintings – more instinctive in its execution Renoir's, more calculated Monet's – have the same motif and the same composition of figures in the landscape: two women at the top of the hill and two at the bottom walking toward us, with the similar effect of creating a sense of movement along the downward sloping path.

▶ **Pierre-Auguste Renoir**, *Path Through the Long Grass*, c. 1874. Musée d'Orsay, Paris.

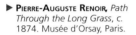

Monet used the bright red of the poppies, with which he dotted the canvas, to augment the overall intensity of his palette. The image is constructed directly out of color and the whole painting is dominated by the marked contrast between the spatial depth suggested by the path through the fields and the total insubstantiality of the rapid brushstrokes, which create vibrant light effects.

Deliberately devoting himself exclusively to the landscape, Monet experimented for a long time with painting in the open air, and tried to give his works the appearance of immediate visions, reproducing on the canvas the fleeting sensations that nature produced on his retina. In his attempt to capture the transient passage of light over the fields, he superimposes dots of pure color that have to be recomposed by the eye of the observer. The result is a picture that, despite its modest size, seems to open a window on the summer countryside and a joyful outdoor life.

The House of the Hanged Man

oil on canvas
21.7 x 26 in / 55 × 66 cm
1873

Faced with the painter's pictures at the first exhibition of the impressionist group in 1874, a critic asked himself: "Shall we mention Cézanne who, by the way, has his own legend? No known jury has ever, even in its dreams, imagined the possibility of accepting a single work by this painter, who came to the Salon carrying his paintings on his back, like Jesus Christ carrying his cross." The critic's reaction to the works of the artist from Aix is not all that surprising, if we remember that even the other painters who took part in the exhibition – and Degas in particular – were reluctant to accept the presence of Cézanne (invited by his friend Camille Pissarro) as they feared the public would be too scandalized by his pictures. Cézanne, whose father saw his initial pessimism about the talents of his son confirmed by the reception given to his first appearance in public, seems to have taken it all with a sense of humor, partly because he at once sold one of the works on show, *The House of the Hanged Man*, to Count Doria, a wealthy landowner with a passion for art. This painting of a striking cottage at Auvers-sur-Oise – where in reality no one had ever hanged himself – has been called the masterpiece of Cézanne's so-called impressionist period. A closer examination will reveal, however, that the artist's research had taken a different direction from that of his friends, as even his contemporaries were aware. The critic Jules Castagnary saw a real danger in Cézanne's works, pointing them out to those who allowed themselves to be carried away by the "impression" as the final and ruinous outcome of their revolutionary experiments: "Cézanne offers a cautionary example of the fate awaiting those who do not ponder and learn. [They] will lapse into an unbridled romanticism, in which nature is only the pretext for daydreams."

Abandoning the harsh and gloomy manner of his early canvases, Cézanne in this period took up painting in the open air, attempting to capture directly the vibrations of light he observed in nature and to adopt the light and rapid touch of the impressionists. But *The House of the Hanged Man* has nothing to do with the fluid landscapes of Monet and Pissarro, apart from the overall composition.

▲ **CAMILLE PISSARRO,** *Red Roofs,* 1877. Musée d'Orsay, Paris.

▼ **CAMILLE PISSARRO,** *Hoarfrost,* 1873. Musée d'Orsay, Paris.

Even in the choice of his subjects Cézanne distinguished himself from the impressionists: his is a solitary landscape, devoid of any human presence and very different, for example, from the pictures of Pissarro, enlivened by the daily labor in the fields, like *Hoarfrost,* shown at the same exhibition in 1874.

In this phase Cézanne first painted a light sketch of the scene, and then went over it here and there with brushstrokes that almost sculpted the canvas and underlined the volumes. The two skeletal trees, the chimneys and the outlines of the roof stand out slightly from the smooth surface of the canvas. The fragmented brushwork and lively palette of colors reflect the influence of Pissarro, but the solid handling of the paint and the rigorous construction of space are characteristics of the painter from Aix.

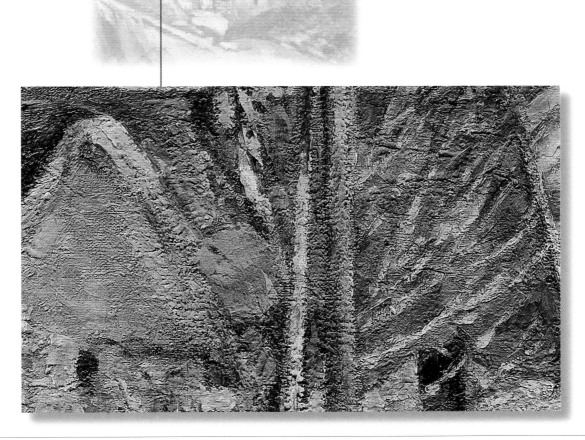

Gustave Caillebotte
(1848 - 1894)
The Floor Planers

oil on canvas
40.2 x 57.7 in / 102 × 146.5 cm
1875

Gustave Caillebotte was a pupil of the academic painter Léon Bonnat, but his admiration for the audacity of the impressionists led him, following his meeting with Monet in 1873, to become one of the group's keenest supporters and patrons. From this moment on he began to help out his friends, buying from them works they thought they would never sell and assembling a collection so large that he was obliged to worry about finding a home for it in the future. In the November of 1876, at the age of just twenty-seven, he made a will in which he left all his pictures to the State on condition that they be housed in the Louvre, and appointed Renoir his executor. Unfortunately, on his death, the State turned down the collection of sixty-seven paintings by the major impressionists and they were denied entry to the Louvre until 1937. Haunted by the presentiment of a premature death, Caillebotte made financial arrangements for another joint exhibition, as he wrote in his will: "It is my wish that sufficient funds be allocated from my estate to finance in 1878, under the best possible conditions, the exhibition of the painters known as the Intransigents or Impressionists." Thanks to his commitment and tenacity the group held its third show in the spring of 1877, "Caillebotte's exhibition" as it was called since he had come up with the funding and supplied many of the works. The picture entitled *The Floor Planers*, rejected by the jury of the official Salon in 1875, was presented at the Impressionist Exhibition of 1876, alongside paintings by Renoir and Monet, as an example of a scene from contemporary life in an interior, to be compared with the sunlit landscapes and views of the two impressionists. Three bare-chested workmen on their knees are planing the floor of a room: the figure on the left is picking up a tool, leading the observer's gaze toward the worker in the middle; the figure on the right has raised his head as if to speak to his companion and the light picks out his features. Buildings and a large patch of the sky are visible through the window in the background, which illuminates the interior.

The scene takes place in a Parisian interior – perhaps Caillebotte's own house, on Rue de Miromesnil – but the artist does not dwell on picturesque details of the setting. The figures of the men, represented from an unusual perspective owing to the decentralized vanishing point and the bold foreshortening that is recurrent in the artist's works, produce a disconcerting effect: they look as if they were sliding toward us along the lines traced on the floor. The almost hyperrealistic representation, poles apart from the images most typical of impressionism, led Émile Zola, while appreciating the theme as a "photograph of reality," to judge its execution too precise and bourgeois. Undoubtedly the thing that most perplexed the public in 1876 was just this "photographic" composition of the scene: receding lines, deformation of the space, unbalanced framing, backlighting. The floor appears to slope downward and the arms to be out of proportion to the torsos.

◀ **GUSTAVE CAILLEBOTTE,**
*On the Pont de l'Europe,
Variation,* c. 1877. Kimbell Art
Museum, Fort Worth.

Like Monet and Manet,
Caillebotte painted several
pictures of this large metal
bridge that spanned the
railroad line leading to the
station of Saint-Lazare.
With this work celebrating
the modernization
of Paris, Gustave
Caillebotte shows us a city
refashioned by the great
works undertaken during
the reign of Napoleon III.

◀ **JEAN-FRANÇOIS MILLET,**
The Angelus, 1858-59.
Musée d'Orsay, Paris.

The subject of *The Floor Planers*, when it was first shown in public, caused a great deal of controversy. In this case, in fact, the painter seems to have joined that distinctly social current of French painting whose aim was to denounce the conditions of the lowest social classes. Two of the most highly rated exponents of this tendency were Jean-François Millet and Jules Bastien-Lepage.

▼ **JULES BASTIEN-LEPAGE,**
Sleeping Peddler, 1882.
Tournai, Musée des Beaux-
Arts.

Pierre-Auguste Renoir
(1841 - 1919)
Nude in the Sunlight

oil on canvas
31.9 x 25.2 in / 81 × 64 cm
1875

Reviewing the second exhibition of the impressionist group in 1876 in Le Figaro, and referring to Renoir's *Nude in the Sunlight* in particular, the critic Albert Wolff wrote in polemically sarcastic tones: "Try to explain to Monsieur Renoir that a woman's torso is not a mass of flesh in the process of decomposition with green and violet spots which denote the state of complete putrefaction of a corpse! […] And this hodgepodge of coarse things is shown in public, without thought of the fatal consequences that may result! Yesterday they arrested, on Rue Peletier, a poor man who had emerged from the exhibition and was biting passersby."
On this occasion Renoir exhibited several important canvases that were to remain among his highest achievements, and that are still some of his best-known paintings today. It is not hard, however, to understand the shock caused by works like *Nude in the Sunlight*, in which there is no drawing or outlines and the natural colors of the flesh are completely distorted by the effects of the light: the public and critics were accustomed to the well-defined forms and lifelike colors of the paintings of the

academic tradition that were exhibited at the Salon and were therefore unprepared for and unresponsive to the tonal research of the painter and his fellow impressionists. The year before the execution of this picture, Renoir had worked for a long time with Claude Monet (his friend since the time of their training under Charles Gleyre) at Argenteuil, on the banks of the Seine: the two painted side by side, with rapid and light brushstrokes, landscapes and figures steeped in the sunlight and reflected in the river. It has been said that impressionism was born precisely out of this study and this attempt to render the reflections of the figures and the vegetation in the water: it was here, in fact, that Renoir developed his enthusiasm for painting *en plein air*, preferring to concentrate, unlike Monet who attempted to represent the pure landscape, on the study of figures in the open. Through the research he conducted in those years he attained that unity between humanity and nature which is characteristic of his most happy period, the impressionist one, in which his instinctive and joyful temperament was able to find free rein.

▶ **PIERRE-AUGUSTE RENOIR,**
The Swing, 1876.
Musée d'Orsay, Paris.

The Swing, like *Nude in the Sunlight*, is the product of studies in the open air, aimed at rendering with immediacy the fleeting effects of sunlight reflected on the woman's skin, on the clothes and hats of the men and on the ground shaded by the trees.

While continuing to mix colors on his palette, Renoir juxtaposed small areas of pure color on the canvas that would be combined, in the eye of the observer, according to precise optical laws, creating an intense luminous vibration. In this way the painter became a virtuoso in the representation of sunlight in the open air, with a sense of joyous immersion in nature. For Renoir, in this phase, there were no points of greater or lesser importance in a painting: the whole canvas was covered with fluid strokes of the brush and spatula, which then fused into a unitary vision impregnated with light.

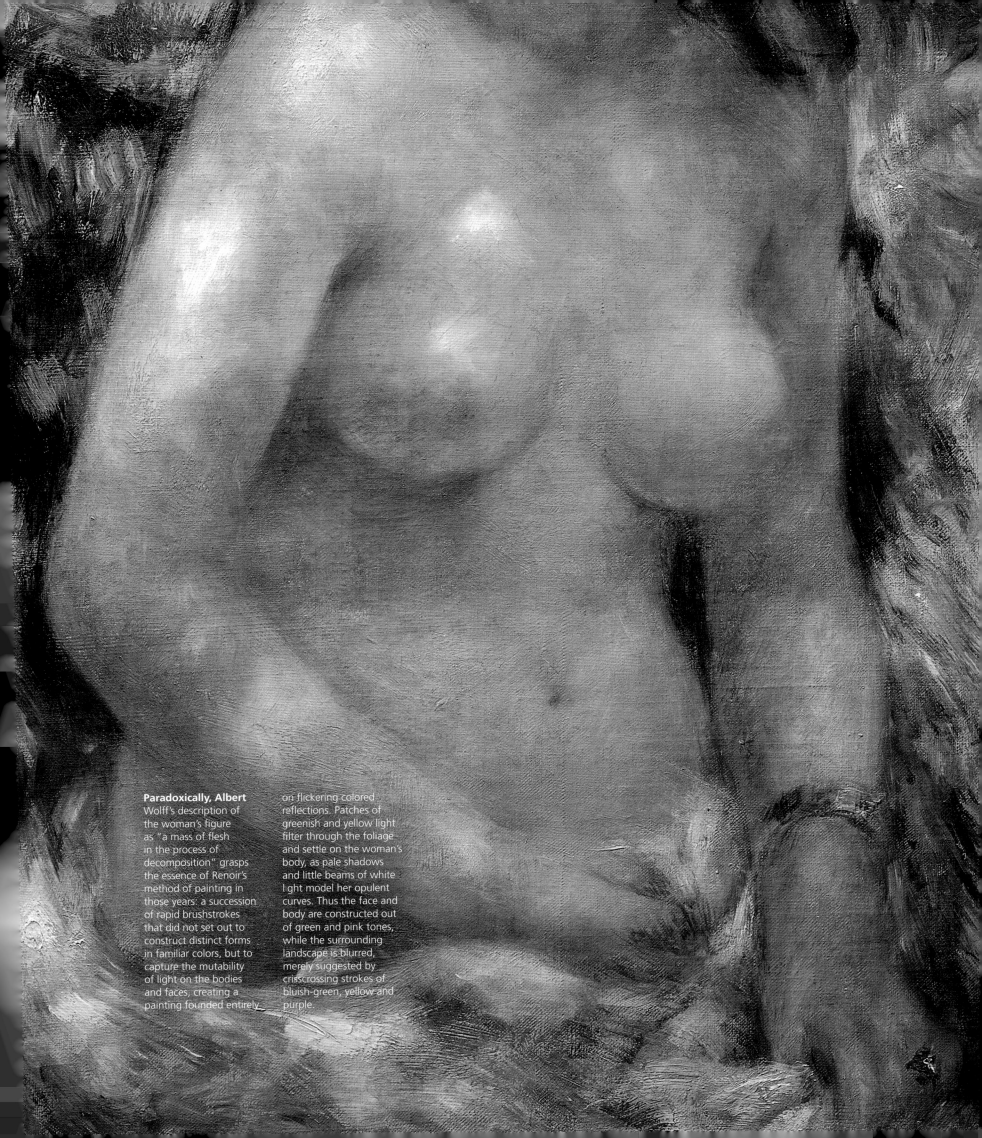

Paradoxically, Albert Wolff's description of the woman's figure as "a mass of flesh in the process of decomposition" grasps the essence of Renoir's method of painting in those years: a succession of rapid brushstrokes that did not set out to construct distinct forms in familiar colors, but to capture the mutability of light on the bodies and faces, creating a painting founded entirely on flickering colored reflections. Patches of greenish and yellow light filter through the foliage and settle on the woman's body, as pale shadows and little beams of white light model her opulent curves. Thus the face and body are constructed out of green and pink tones, while the surrounding landscape is blurred, merely suggested by crisscrossing strokes of bluish-green, yellow and purple.

Edgar Degas
(1834 - 1917)

Absinthe

oil on canvas
36.2 x 26.8 in / 92 × 68 cm
1876

A bohemian and a poor prostitute stupefied with alcohol look as if they are imprisoned in the narrow space between the table and the seat in a Parisian café, in front of two full glasses and an empty bottle. In the society of the Third Republic the motif of the proletariat seeking escape from a soul-destroying existence in the bottle – and especially in absinthe, which became a literary myth – was one of the most frequently represented by painters as well as writers. In 1877 Zola's novel *L'Assommoir (The Drunkard)*, which presented the problem of alcoholism in the working-class district of Goutte d'Or as a social evil that needed to be combated, met with huge success. Alcoholism among women, in particular, was to attract growing public attention. A treatise by Devoisins (1885) emphatically declared that "the alcoholism of women constitutes the greatest threat to society of our time": it led to sterility and prostitution and was even capable of compromising national security. Yet the depiction of two such degraded human specimens – for which the actress Ellen Andrée and the engraver Marcellin Desboutin, a famous bohemian of the day, posed as models – in *Absinthe* had no polemical intent. Notwithstanding the scandal caused by its exhibition in London in 1893 – which persuaded its first purchaser to resell the work to the collector Isaac de Camondo, who brought it back to France – Degas did not paint the picture as a denunciation, but as a *tranche de vie*, a typical scene of the Parisian cafés, set in the Nouvelle Athènes, one of the favorite haunts of the impressionist group. What interested the painter was psychological analysis of the two figures, from which any communication and any element that slips into the anecdotal are absent: in short it is an impressionistic snapshot of an aspect of contemporary life.

Although an
impressionist picture in both its intention and its theme of Parisian life, *Absinthe* is remote from the festive motifs and bright colors of the impressionists in its somber tones and the density of the paint. By blurring the surroundings of the figures, Degas throws their faces into relief, focusing attention on the unhealthy pallor of the woman and the ruddy vulgarity of the man. The dark reflections of their heads in the mirror on the wall help to accentuate the sense of isolation of one from the other.

The unusual point of
view, the apparently squashed position of the pair and the arrangement of the table make the image look like part of a larger composition, as if it were a photograph. Degas had no hesitation in using photography as an aid, for its ability to reveal aspects or moments of reality that escape the eye: the painting was also intended to make visible things that the eye does not see, offering an instantaneous image in line with the aims of impressionism.

Degas's *Absinthe* was
to serve as a model for
similar themes tackled
in *fin-de-siècle* painting.
See for example Henri de
Toulouse-Lautrec's *The
Drinker*, another "slice
of life" representing a
woman seated in front
of a glass, with a lost
expression and her body
crumpled by the effect of
alcohol.

PIERRE-AUGUSTE RENOIR
(1841 - 1919)

Dance at the Moulin de la Galette

oil on canvas
51.6 x 68.9 in / 131 × 175 cm
1876

In the spring of 1876, Renoir's friends helped him to carry the canvas every day from his studio on Rue Cortot, in Montmartre, where he had moved to be closer to the subject he wanted to paint, to the Moulin de la Galette, not very far from the studio but still fairly difficult to get to with an object of this size. In those years the Moulin was a meeting place with a respectable reputation, where the local inhabitants and the numerous artists who had come to live in the area used to go to have a good time and dance. Renoir was excited by the prospect of capturing the joyful atmosphere of a petit bourgeois dance hall and, through it, the carefree society of his time, *la vie moderne* extolled by Baudelaire in his writings on art. The friends and chance passersby who pose for the artist are presentably dressed, in sober neckties and patent-leather shoes; they are the new heroes of contemporary life. The vision that Renoir presents of the world to which he belongs is an optimistic one. His painting seems to exorcize the problematic aspects of daily life, and not coincidentally would be defined by the critics as "romantic impressionism" for its poetic tone of gaiety and for the subjects represented: lovers at a dance or in a garden, gatherings of friends at Bougival or Chatou, the localities on the outskirts of the city preferred by Parisians for their Sunday outings. The *Dance at the Moulin de la Galette* is the masterpiece of this style, in which he appears to have fully attained the dissolution of form sought by the impressionists, founded on the technique of laying on pure colors in small touches filled with light. As is well known, this technique and its results were not understood by the critics, who did not fail to attack the painting, pouring ridicule in particular on the insubstantiality of the dance floor, "a surface resembling the violet clouds that obscure the sky on a stormy day." Only the critic Georges Rivière grasped the true value of the work, describing it in enthusiastic terms as "a page of history, a precious monument of Parisian life depicted with rigorous exactness."

What interested Renoir when painting *en plein air* was not, as in the case of Claude Monet, nature in itself, the light that it contained and reflected, but the effect it had on figures, the colors that bodies and faces took on when illuminated by sunlight filtering through leaves. Thus the particular version of impressionism proposed by Renoir was a move in the direction of a new conception of the landscape, no longer in the role of the protagonist but subordinated to the figures that were reflected in it.

▲ **CLAUDE MONET,** *The Rocks at Pourville, Low Tide*, 1882. Memorial Art Gallery of the University of Rochester, New York.

▶ **CLAUDE MONET,** *Autumn at Argenteuil*, 1873. Courtauld Institute, London.

▶ **PIERRE-AUGUSTE RENOIR,** *Under the Trees at the Moulin de la Galette*, 1876. Pushkin Museum, Moscow.

At the time he was getting ready to work on the *Dance at the Moulin de la Galette* Renoir painted *Under the Trees*. Going to live in Montmartre, he studied the atmosphere, the light and the faces and began to produce a series of sketches. He also painted, in the same fragmented and luminous style, this amorous scene, observed by a female figure who, judging by the similarity of the dress and hairstyle, may be Estelle, the model who was to pose in the foreground of the *Dance*.

▼ **ÉDOUARD MANET,** *Claude Monet and His Wife on the Floating Studio*, 1874. Neue Pinakothek, Munich.

During the period that Renoir and Monet spent together at Argenteuil, Monet was able to use a boat, a true floating studio and big enough to sleep on, where he liked to isolate himself to observe the effects of light on the water from dawn to dusk. Renoir preferred to paint in company, at Montmartre, surrounded by the bustle of the crowd and dancing couples.

The space of the picture is constructed entirely from tones and colors, which translate the effects of the light into a whirling movement: it is remarkable that Renoir employs neither dark tones not shadows, but color alone to render the reflection of the sun on the faces and clothes of the figures and on the pink- and blue-tinted ground. Many of the artist's friends posed as models for the dancers and for the group of painters in the foreground, huddled around Georges Rivière, the first on the right and a critic very well disposed toward Renoir. Also in the foreground, seated on the bench, is the model Estelle and, to the left, Margot, the model who was most in demand at that moment, dancing with the Spanish painter Pedro Vidal de Solares y Cardenas.

CAMILLE PISSARRO
(1830 - 1903)

Red Roofs

oil on canvas
21.5 x 25.8 in / 54.5 × 65.6 cm
1877

Camille Pissarro painted *Red Roofs* more than twenty years after he moved to France from the Danish West Indies, where he was born. In 1855 the great Universal Exposition had just opened its doors in Paris, offering an unrivaled panorama of artistic production to a young man who had chosen to devote his life to painting. On that occasion, however, it was not the celebrated and eternally clashing personalities of Delacroix and Ingres that caught Pissarro's attention, nor the scandal caused by Courbet's Pavillon du Réalisme, but the few landscapes shown by Camille Corot and François Daubigny. The influence of these artists, who worked at Barbizon, near the forest of Fontainebleau, was decisive in emancipating Pissarro from the academic style and persuading him to paint almost nothing but landscapes. It was he, in turn, who urged his own friends to lighten their palettes, to emerge from their studios and paint from life and, finally, to organize the first exhibition of the impressionist group. *Red Roofs* testifies perfectly, on the one hand, to Pissarro's predilection for the French countryside, and on the other to his relationship with Paul Cézanne. In fact after the Franco-Prussian War of 1870 Pissarro, who was particularly fond of that sort of great market garden that extended around Paris, with its cultivated fields and hardworking inhabitants, living in harmony with the rhythms of nature, settled at Pontoise, where the hills, the land and the river offered him a wide variety of subjects. He was joined there in 1873 by Paul Cézanne, and the two painters worked side by side. As Pissarro acknowledged later, he had at one and the same time influenced his friend and been influenced by him: it is possible to discern, in the solid construction and vivid coloring of *Red Roofs*, the effects of this fertile exchange.

In *Red Roofs* Pissarro uses a richer palette than the dark tints of his early years: no longer does he reproduce the real colors of the objects, but the ones he feels necessary to the harmony of the picture. The deep blue of the sky is echoed in the windows of the houses; the intense red in the fields is not found in nature, but resonates with the color of the roofs. Such bright colors were not immediately welcomed and the critic Albert Wolff wrote: "Try to make Monsieur Pissarro understand that trees are not violet; that the sky is not the color of fresh butter; that the things he paints can be seen in no country; and that no sensible human being could countenance such aberrations."

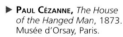

At Pontoise Pissarro and Cézanne depicted the same landscapes *en plein air*, painting alongside one another as Cézanne's sketch of his friend on his way to work testifies.

▼ **Paul Cézanne,** *Pissarro on His Way to Work*, 1872. Cabinet des Dessins, Musée du Louvre, Paris.

▶ **Paul Cézanne,** *The House of the Hanged Man*, 1873. Musée d'Orsay, Paris.

In *Red Roofs* the trees are no longer a simple element of the landscape but, forming a screen between the foreground and the buildings, underline the structure of the composition and reinforce it, an effect very similar to Cézanne's *The House of the Hanged Man*. In fact this picture was painted following the two artists' stay at Pontoise.

The markedly horizontal axis constituted by the fields and the contour of the hill is counterbalanced by the roofs of the houses. This aspect of the composition is reminiscent of the landscapes painted by Pissarro at Pontoise: for example the *Hermitage at Pontoise*, in which the countryside in the environs of Paris is described using similar methods.

▲ Camille Pissarro, *The Hermitage at Pontoise*, 1873. Musée d'Orsay, Paris.

PIERRE PUVIS DE CHAVANNES
(1824 - 1898)

The Poor Fisherman

oil on canvas
61 x 75.8 in / 155 × 192.5 cm
1881

This picture captivated the public and critics, but it also caused a fair amount of perplexity, as is clear from the words of one observer: "I've seen a lot of poor fishermen, but never one like Monsieur Puvis de Chavannes's. He had a pipe and a cap. I've seen fisherman's wives too, but they weren't dressed in a sheet and weren't picking flowers." The bewildering effect that the work still has today stems from the enigmatic character of the subject, for which innumerable interpretations in a symbolist key have been put forward, all of them very far from the artist's intentions: some saw it as a grand allegory of the human condition, others as an image of faith in the divine and hope in the regeneration of life. Puvis was obliged to explain personally that it was simply a picture of a widowed fisherman and his two children, and so, if people really wanted to assign it a more general significance, the work was a representation of suffering. In fact, even though his painting exercised a considerable influence on the emerging current of symbolism, the artist remained independent of it: the picture is a touching image of human loneliness, quiet and simple but with a powerful impact. Thus the painting remained isolated in the context of the art of the time, as it was impossible to assign it to a particular school or category: Puvis's style is neither symbolist, nor realist, nor historical, nor allegorical.

And this is where the revolutionary character of *The Poor Fisherman* lies: in the absence of a clear-cut subject and in the monumental essentiality of the composition, which excludes any link with the pictures of ancient history, the meticulous landscapes or the genre scenes with a taste for the anecdotal that could be seen at the Salons of his day. It is revealing that the work received an enthusiastic reception from young artists, who recognized Puvis from this moment on as a genuine "classic"; it was also the first of the artist's paintings to enter a national museum.

Movement and action are totally missing from the work: what holds sway is a sense of emptiness, of silence. The scene seems to be set in a timeless atmosphere: the fisherman withdrawn into his own sorrow appears to concentrate within himself both the poetry of the ancient myths and the gloomy thoughts of modern man.

The landscape that surround him is desolate, his boat floats on a river with turbid waters. The sensation of abandonment conveyed by this image is not rhetoric; nor does it carry a social message. Puvis does not describe the condition of that particular fisherman, but creates a universal image, in which all men can recognize themselves.

▲ **Pierre Puvis de Chavannes,**
Young Girls at the Seaside,
1879. Musée d'Orsay, Paris.

The stark monumentality
without rhetoric of
The Poor Fisherman
can also be found in
the *Young Girls at the
Seaside*, in which the pale
colors and the modular
harmony of the lines
suggest an atmosphere
of gloomy peace that
leaves room, once again,
for interpretations in a
symbolist key.

The Poor Fisherman
caught the imagination of
critics, poets and men of
letters and exercised an
enormous influence on
painters, many of whom
copied it or were inspired
by it: from Maillol to
Seurat, and from Gauguin
to Picasso. Puvis used
unusual means for the
time to give the image its
emotional force: a very
limited range of colors,
the absence of shading
or relief in the figures
and a representation of
the landscape that was
not "photographic" or
descriptive, but aimed to
summarize and "flatten."

P. Puvis de Chavannes

AUGUSTE RODIN
(1840 - 1917)

Ugolino and His Sons

plaster
55.1 x 55.1 in / 140 × 140 cm
1882

In the 33rd canto of the *Inferno* (71-5) Dante recounts the slow and atrocious death of a man – Count Ugolino della Gherardesca, the former ruler of Pisa – imprisoned and condemned to die of hunger with his sons, in these lines: "I saw the three fall, one by one, between / The fifth day and the sixth; whence I betook me, / Already blind, to groping over each, / And three days called them after they were dead; / Then hunger did what sorrow could not do." It is on these despairing last words of Ugolino that Rodin lingers in his representation of the tragic episode, which had taken place in 1289.

In 1880 Edmond Turquet, Undersecretary for the Fine Arts and an enthusiastic admirer of Rodin, commissioned from him a bronze door decorated with scenes from Dante's *Divina Commedia* in bas-relief for Paris's new museum of decorative arts. The door would become the *Gates of Hell*, one of the most creative works of art of the modern era.

The museum, which was to be built on the ruins of the Cour des Comptes (the site on which the Gare d'Orsay would later rise instead) was never constructed, but the *Gates of Hell* became the hub of Rodin's artistic activity up until his death, the motivation for many of his most important sculptures and the proving ground for his lively imagination. In 1906 the intensely dramatic figures of Ugolino and his sons were slightly modified, enlarged and, cloaked in ample drapery, used to form an independent group.

Neither mythological nor biblical, the subject of the work had no models in the academic tradition and therefore permitted the artist great freedom. Rodin, passionately fond of Dante since the early 1870s, reinterpreted the story from a romantic perspective: he represented Ugolino as an embodiment of man transformed into beast by suppression of his conscience, caught in the act of clambering over the corpses of his children as if to devour them.

Another artist, Jean-Baptiste Carpeaux (1827-75), had tackled the theme of Count Ugolino in sculpture before Rodin. In 1854, after winning the Prix de Rome, Carpeaux had been able to go to Italy, where he carved the group of *Ugolino and His Sons*. Rodin admired this work, whose final version was exhibited at the Salon of 1862 and then erected, following its acquisition by the State, in the garden of the Tuileries. But Carpeaux's sculpture adhered to the traditional rules, with a pyramidal composition in which Ugolino dominates the group of four sons, whereas Rodin adopted a far more original scheme, articulated in curved lines in which the forms almost seem to be enclosed within themselves.

At the very moment of the signing of the contract for the *Gates of Hell*, a long article in the *Revue des Deux Mondes* held up the names of Dante and Michelangelo as models of vigor and moral integrity, capable of expressing pitiless judgments of their contemporaries.

So it is significant that Rodin should have adopted the *Last Judgment* in the Sistine Chapel as a model for the composition of his door. And Rodin's undertaking can in fact be compared with that of Michelangelo, especially in its ambitious complexity.

To accentuate the horror of the scene, the sculptor modeled precisely the protagonist's face, distorted with madness, and represented in detail the anatomy of his vigorous body, the muscles taught with effort, as if to reveal the evidence of an inhuman vitality.

Pierre-Auguste Renoir
(1841 - 1919)

Dance in the Country

oil on canvas
70.9 x 35.4 in / 180 × 90 cm
1882 - 1883

For all the artists of the impressionist group the beginning of the eighties was a period of reflection, and for some of crisis. Renoir in particular, after his journey to Italy in 1882, started to question the value of his activity as a painter.

It is likely that Émile Zola had contributed to this with the criticism he had made of impressionist painting in 1880. Although he had been one of its earliest supporters, he now accused it of incompleteness, extremism and the inability to create a truly original style. Above all, however, Renoir had seen the masters of the Renaissance in Rome, and was especially struck by Raphael: dissatisfied with his own works as an artist, Renoir was induced by this experience to confer a greater solidity on his painting, to take more care over the composition and to adopt a simpler way of laying on the paint than the complicated technique used by the impressionists, linked to the immediate reproduction of what they

saw. From this time on, and up until his death, he was to paint mostly bathers – and thus tackle the female nude, the most classic theme in painting – and figures of women that, depicted with dense brushwork, have the imposing force of sculptures.

Dance in the Country was one of the first products of this new period of "reconquest of form."

In 1882 Paul Durand-Ruel, the art dealer who was the first to handle the works of the impressionists, commissioned from Renoir two large pictures on the theme of dance in the city and the country: these were among the last works that the painter devoted to the amusements of the Parisian people.

The models who posed for the painting were Paul Lothe and Renoir's future wife, Aline Charigot, radiant and extroverted. It presents an idyllic image of life in the country, where spontaneity prevails over the formal conventions that govern social relations in the city.

▲ **RAPHAEL,** *Triumph of Galatea,*
1511. Villa Farnesina, Rome.

▼ **PIERRE-AUGUSTE RENOIR,** *Dance
at the Moulin de la Galette,*
1876. Musée d'Orsay, Paris.

The predominance of
the figures of the dancers
over the setting is a
consequence of Renoir's
visit to Italy, where he had
been greatly impressed by
the solidly defined forms
of ancient Roman art and
the classical drawing of
Raphael, especially in the
frescoes in Villa Farnesina.
Rather than on the
evocation of an ambience,
of its light and tonalities,
as in the *Dance at the
Moulin de la Galette*, a
fully impressionist work,
Renoir concentrates
here on the precise and
vigorous definition of the
human, and especially the
female figure, against a
backdrop that is barely
suggested.

◄ **PIERRE-AUGUSTE RENOIR**, *Dance in the City*, 1883. Musée d'Orsay, Paris.

To the uninhibited and animated poses of the *Dance in the Country*, and the rather gaudy party dress worn by the woman, the *Dance in the City* contrasts the sober elegance and measured attitudes of high Parisian society. In her memoirs, the painter Suzanne Valadon, who posed for this picture, related that Renoir went with her to the dressmaker and chose the dress she was to wear, a fact symptomatic of the extreme attention the painter paid to the composition of his canvases. The carefully chosen evening gown, pearl white with touches of pink and blue, allowed Renoir to execute an extraordinary piece of painting, almost virtuoso in its sumptuous representation of the fabric. Even the choice of the marble half column in the background is not coincidental, but appears to be an explicit allusion to the painting of the Renaissance.

Woman with a Parasol Turned to the Left

oil on canvas
51.6 x 34.6 in / 131 × 88 cm
1886

In 1886, the year of the last joint exhibition by the impressionists, Émile Zola published his novel *L'Œuvre* (*The Masterpiece*), telling the story of a painter, called Claude, during the years of the movement's struggle for acceptance: a talented but crazy artist, devastated by the conflict between his grand dreams and the insufficiency of his creative powers, who brings his life to a tragic end by committing suicide. The publication of the novel seems to have accelerated the progressive disintegration of the impressionist group. Cézanne, who recognized himself in this figure, immediately broke with Zola, even though their friendship dated from their high-school days in Aix-en-Provence. Monet, Pissarro and Renoir also saw in the novel a betrayal of their hopes and a lack of understanding of their research and distanced themselves from the writer who, having achieved success, now stood in judgment on the friends he considered a failure. Many of the group decided to leave Paris and this separation seems to have accentuated the independence of the directions they took in their art: Cézanne went back to Aix-en-Provence for good. Pissarro, already focused on his experiments with divisionism, had also gone to live in the provinces, while Renoir achieved his first major success with a one-man show at the Galerie Georges Petit. For his part Monet had settled at Giverny, a village halfway between Paris and Rouen, in 1883, and it was here that he painted *Woman with a Parasol*. He had already tried his hand at figure painting in the years between 1865 and 1868 (in *Le Déjeuner sur l'herbe* and *Women in the Garden*), always portraying friends and acquaintances. Once, around 1888, on the advice of Renoir, he had hired a model in Paris to come to Giverny to pose for him, but immediately had to give up the idea as Madame Hoschedé, his companion and future second wife, announced that if the model were to set foot in their house, she was going to leave. Consequently Monet's studies of figures are never posed, but moments drawn from real life, in line with the anti-academic principles to which the painter always sought to remain faithful.

◄ CLAUDE MONET, *Woman with a Parasol Turned to the Right*, 1886. Musée d'Orsay, Paris.

The two versions of the *Woman with a Parasol* are an attempt to translate a fleeting vision into painting with immediacy: they cannot be described as portraits as the two female figures have no individualized features and their faces, hidden by the veil or the shadow of the parasol, are barely sketched and unrecognizable. As if surprised on a stroll, they turn abruptly and the veils of their hats fly like weathervanes indicating the direction of the wind. The dark and distinct shadow of the woman on the meadow has vanished in the second version; the colors are more delicate and transparent and the figure appears to blend into the surroundings, rendering it even more graceful and elegant. In the first picture, on the other hand, the forms are more defined, although here too the shadows are luminous and the strokes of the brush extremely light.

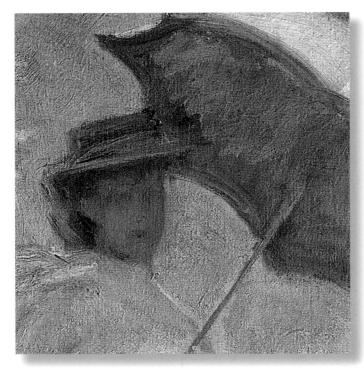

The light comes from the right, like the clouds that seem to be driven by the wind.
The horizontal plane on which the woman stands appears to be contrasted by the rapid vertical brushstrokes used to depict the grass and the other plants in bending

in the breeze. The painter Berthe Morisot declared that when looking at Monet's pictures she always knew "which way I would have turned my parasol," indicating the atmospheric precision of the effects of light and "wind" in her friend's paintings.

 **PIERRE-AUGUSTE RENOIR,** *Lise with Umbrella*, 1867. Folkwang Museum, Essen.

A comparison with an early portrait by Renoir, *Lise with Umbrella*, painted twenty years before Monet's, reveals the essence of the revolution of painting *en plein air*. The appearance

of Monet's female figures is transformed by their surroundings, whereas in Renoir's picture they serve solely as a backdrop to a posed portrait, executed in the studio. Monet has depicted the woman with immediacy, capturing the enchantment of a bright summer day.

The Talisman (Landscape at the Bois d'Amour at Pont-Aven)

oil on wood
10.6 x 8.7 in / 27 × 22 cm
1888

The birth of the Nabis movement is traditionally dated to 1888, the year in which Paul Sérusier showed his friends the *Bois d'Amour*, painted at Pont-Aven on the lid of a cigar box. At the village of Pont-Aven, in Brittany, the young painter had met Paul Gauguin, who had been generous with his advice: "How do you see that tree? Is it really green? Then put green in, the most beautiful green in your palette. And that shadow, isn't it rather blue? Then don't be afraid of painting it as blue as possible." Maurice Denis was later to stress the importance of Gauguin's teaching to the development of a group awareness and shared aesthetic among the Nabis: "Thus we learned that a work of art is nothing but a transposition, an exaggeration, the passionate equivalent of a sensation received." Such a statement, if considered alongside Sérusier's little picture, is a decided stand against the presuppositions of imitation of nature that were common to traditional painting and to impressionism.

Sérusier's landscape was immediately dubbed *The Talisman* by Gauguin's very young followers, who regarded it not as a mere sketch, but as an almost magical work, a small treasure rich in hidden meanings that could open up new horizons in the world of art for them. And in fact that is what it did: the newly formed group liked to surround itself with esoteric rites of initiation and pose as a secret society (the name came from the Hebrew word *navi*, a "prophet" or "seer").

The story of the Nabis movement was to last until 1900, the date of their final exhibition at the Galerie Bernheim-Jeune in Paris. Over this brief span of time they carried out a true joint artistic project, rooted in the superseding of any naturalism and its replacement by swirls and flourishes, laden with symbols; critical with regard to the hierarchy of artistic genres, they also devoted themselves to the decorative arts, sculpture, literature, stage design and illustration.

Maurice Denis's famous definition of the work of art as a "flat surface covered with colors assembled in a certain order" could not be more apt for this small picture. The violence of the colors placed side by side without gradations revolutionizes the traditional representation of reality, including that of the impressionists: we are not dealing here with a copy of nature, but a transposition of the emotions to which it gives rise into colors. The subject (a wood) is at bottom irrelevant, a pretext for the cunning combination of areas of color to create an overall harmony.

A representation of a wood like this, defined moreover by its author as "sacred," implies a sensibility linked more closely to the dimension of dream than to a recognizable real model. It does, however, seem possible to recognize the wood: yellow and blue patches lined up along a path are reflected, together with a house, in the waters of a lake.

VINCENT VAN GOGH
(1853 - 1890)

Self-Portrait

oil on canvas
25.6 x 21.5 in / 65 × 54.5 cm
1889

Vincent – as he liked to sign his canvases – moved from Paris to Arles, in the South of France, in February 1888, and it was during the two years he spent there that he produced the greater part of his work. His dream was to create with Paul Gauguin (who prudently backed out of the project) a "Studio of the South," where the very foundations of art could be renewed by taking the premises of impressionism to their extreme consequences. After the dramatic conclusion of Gauguin's stay (Van Gogh cut off the lobe of his own ear following a violent argument), the painter began to experience the periodic crises of mental instability that led him, in May 1888, to decide to have himself committed to an asylum at Saint-Rémy. Here he continued to work at a frantic pace, and in September of the following year, given the shortage of models, painted his self-portrait several times. He wrote from Arles to his brother Theo: "The emotions are sometimes so strong that one works without being aware of working [...] and the strokes come with a sequence and coherence like words in a speech or a letter." The comparison could not have been more apt. In such moments of inspiration he painted in the way other people write: just as the marks left by the pen on the paper in a handwritten manuscript reveal the state of mind of the writer, Van Gogh's brushstrokes tell us something about his emotions, about the creative frenzy that possessed him at the moment in which he set them on the canvas. In the self-portraits he interrogates himself, and the progress of his illness: here he shows us his pinched face and his penetrating gaze, staring into space, that seems to be glowering at his own image. The splendid blue background expresses the artist's inner torment through the whirling pattern of the brushstrokes. This is the greatest innovation of an art in which the colors and forms of the objects are transformed instinctively by the artist's sensibility.

▲ **VINCENT VAN GOGH,**
The Potato Eaters, 1885.
Rijksmuseum Kröller-Müller,
Otterlo.

Van Gogh began his
career as a preacher
among the miners of the
Borinage region, but was
expelled by the official
Church. Yet he did not

lose his conviction that it
was his mission to act as
a guide for the have-nots,
for the exploited workers
and peasants whom he
started to portray in his
paintings. *The Potato
Eaters* can be regarded
as the epitome of this
early Dutch period. He

explained the meaning of
the painting in a letter:
"I have tried to make it
clear how those people,
eating their potatoes
under the lamplight,
have dug the earth with
those very hands they
put in their dish, and so
[the picture] speaks of

manual labor, and how
they have honestly earned
their food. I have wanted
to give the impression
of quite a different way
of living than that of us
civilized people. Therefore
I am not at all anxious for
everyone to like it or to
admire it at once."

The uniform tonality
of the painting is an
intense blue which, barely
flecked with white, gray,
green and mauve, gives
the image a breathtaking
vivacity. The eyes with
which the artist scrutinizes
himself are the focal point
of the work; the prickly
roughness of the beard is
represented by a bristling
mass of dry and hard
brushstrokes; the pale
face is veiled with bluish
tints on pink.

◀ **VINCENT VAN GOGH,**
Self-Portrait, 1887.
Musée d'Orsay, Paris.

In the *Self-Portrait* painted
two years earlier the
procedure is similar: Van
Gogh uses the brush not
just to color, but also to
draw and to lay the paint
on in thick layers. It can be
said that he constructs the
picture through the use
of a heavy impasto, giving
the image a real texture.
In the background, where,
as always, there is no hint
of a setting, the already
rapid rhythm of the
brushstrokes grows dizzy,
transforming the picture
into a mesh of lines
animated by a feverish
vitality.

Henri de Toulouse-Lautrec
(1864 - 1901)
La Toilette

oil and turpentine on cardboard
26.4 x 21.3 in / 67 × 54 cm
1889

One morning, after a night of merrymaking, Henri de Toulouse-Lautrec took his group of friends, all still in evening dress, to Mademoiselle Dihau who, with some hesitation, let them into her modest apartment. Here the painter showed his friends the paintings by Degas hanging on the walls and ordered them to kneel in front of them in obeisance. Even under less eccentric circumstances, Toulouse-Lautrec frequently went to the home of Marie Dihau and her brother Désiré – musicians who collected Degas's works – to listen to good music and admire the pictures of the man he considered his master. And it was there that the young man finally met the elderly painter, receiving from him praise of which Degas was normally very sparing. Later, Toulouse-Lautrec would describe this as "the best encouragement I ever received." Wealthy scion of one of the oldest noble families in France and typical figure of the *peintre maudit*, addicted to alcohol and nightlife and defiant of social and artistic conventions, Toulouse-Lautrec chose as the models of his painting the actress-singers, "female clowns" and prostitutes of Montmartre.

Posing for him on this occasion is a woman with red hair, seated half-naked on the floor with her back to the observer: the unusual subject, pose and point of view cannot help but recall Degas. As in the latter's work, moreover, the representation of a scene of female intimacy is not presented in a voyeuristic manner and does not linger over the details of the setting, but is an opportunity for a study of the nude, of perspective and of light. Such an accurate nude study is particularly important, for it has been observed that the true protagonist of all Toulouse-Lautrec's work is the human body.

In fact, especially in the swirling lines of his advertising posters, the human silhouette became the fundamental form of expression of a new style that would come to be known as art nouveau: a style of which Toulouse-Lautrec laid the first foundations.

The figure of the woman viewed from behind, common in Toulouse-Lautrec's work (another example is the *Woman at the Window* in the Albi museum), owes a great deal to Degas's pastels. In *The Tub*, for instance, we find the same elevated point of view and an inverted perspective that confuses the observer's perception of the space. Degas's image is more daring in its composition than Toulouse-Lautrec's *Woman at the Window*, which has a more traditional structure.

Degas and Toulouse-Lautrec painted numerous scenes of women in the intimacy of their homes; for Degas these were above all studies of the postures and attitudes of the human body. If we compare these two works with a similar subject, in which the model is portrayed in the act of combing her hair in front of a mirror: Toulouse-Lautrec, unlike Degas, is interested in studying the expression on the woman's face, to which he gives grotesque features, almost those of a caricature.

The work is rapidly executed and must have been painted directly from life, given that there are no preliminary studies. The brushwork is fibrous, with blue-violet lines that define the figure of the woman, lightened in the flesh tones and on the hair by touches of yellow and orange.

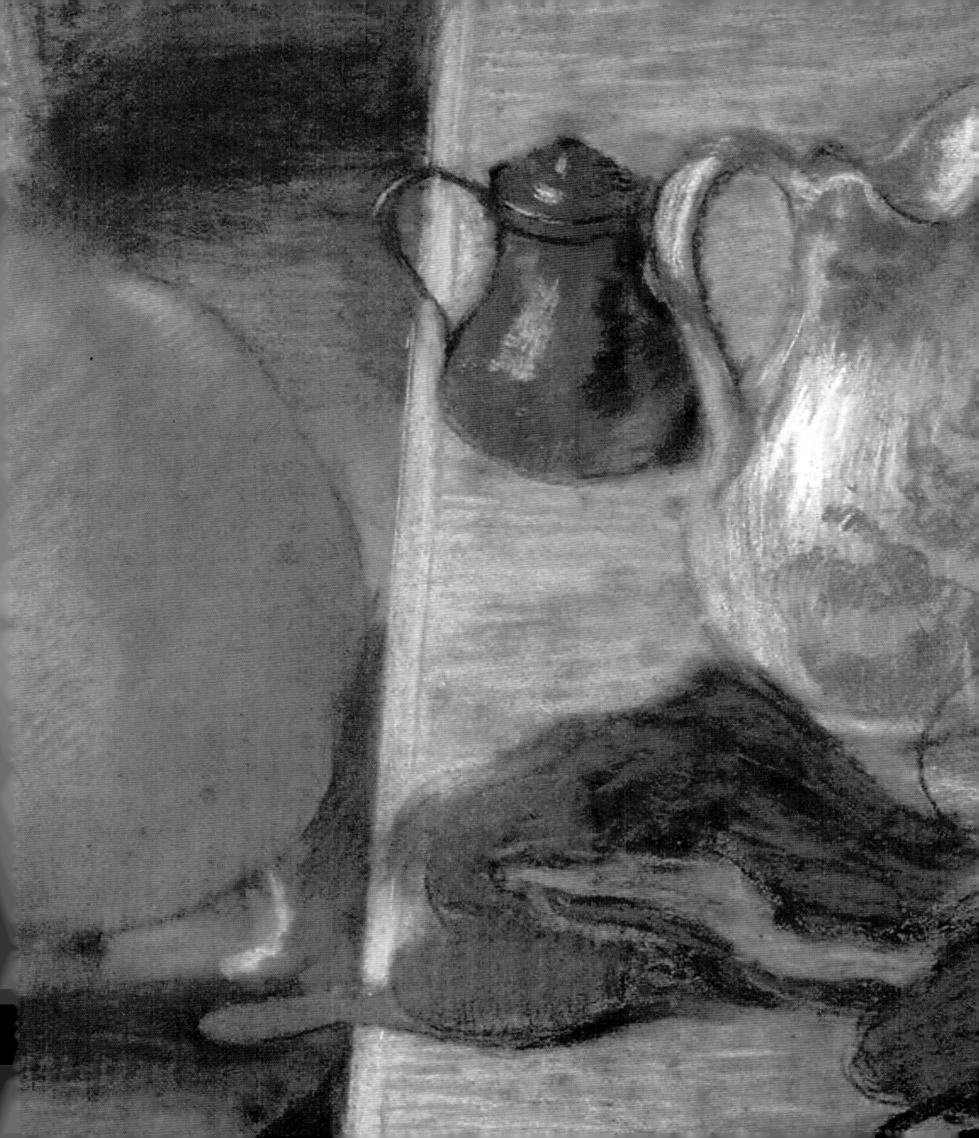

Paul Gauguin
(1848 - 1903)

La belle Angèle

oil on canvas
36.2 x 28.7 in / 92 × 73 cm
1889

When, at the end of her sittings in the summer of 1889, Marie Angélique Satre, considered one of the most beautiful women in Pont-Aven, was finally able to see her portrait (Gauguin had arrived that morning full of satisfaction and excitement, looking for the best place to hang it), she exclaimed in horror "how dreadful!" and refused to have it in the house. Gauguin was hurt, as he thought it his most successful portrait. His disappointment came on top of the setback he had suffered a few days earlier when, showing the work to friends and colleagues, he had received only not very flattering criticism. Later the picture would be bought by Degas, an enthusiastic collector of Gauguin's work, and on his death would be donated to the State by the art dealer Ambroise Vollard. Paul Gauguin's life was a sort of uninterrupted journey: his search for the origins – his own and of art – led him to travel several times from Brittany to Oceania.

In 1886 he went for the first time to Pont-Aven, a picturesque Breton village that had been home to a cosmopolitan colony of artists since the 1860s. In 1888 he returned there after a visit to Martinique, and wrote: "I love Brittany. I find there the savage, the primitive. When my wooden shoes reverberate on this granite soil, I hear the muffled, heavy and powerful note I am seeking in painting." After a stay in Arles with Van Gogh, which came to a dramatic end when the two men fell out, he went back to Pont-Aven and painted *La belle Angèle*, a title which he wrote in capital letters on the canvas. The model's reaction to her finished picture is not surprising: the stiff pose and fixed expression that the painter bestowed on her give the figure traits that might seem caricatural but which actually, together with the Breton costume worn on feast days and the ceramic object in the shape of a human being to the left of the model, lend the image a solemn character, almost that of a sacred symbol.

It was at Pont-Aven
that Gauguin met
the painter Émile
Bernard, an encounter
that was decisive for
the development of
the technique called
cloisonnisme, in which
La belle Angèle was
a fundamental stage.
Inspired by the medieval
art of stained glass,
cloisonnisme envisaged
the use of large areas
of flat and contrasting
color, separated by thick
outlines (like the arc
of a circle that frames
Angélique). The end result
is particularly decorative
and abstract, an explicit
rejection of any imitation
of reality.

▶ **PAUL GAUGUIN,** *Breton Peasant Women*, 1894. Musée d'Orsay, Paris.

Bernard was to paint several pictures of Breton women, as did Gauguin himself. During his last stay in Brittany, thanks to the influence of the colors and the women he had seen on the island of Tahiti, he would create a composition of extraordinary monumentality in *Breton Peasant Women*.

Taking an approach often used by Japanese painters, Gauguin chose a wholly unnatural layout for the picture, inserting the woman's bust in a sort of round window that separates the figure from the background. The two spaces of the image are delimited by the arc of a circle traced by an ocher line: this, combined with the wallpaper-like effect of the background (which consists not of a naturalistic landscape but a flat, blue surface with applications of pink and light blue flowers), confers a markedly decorative character on the picture.

▶ **PAUL GAUGUIN,** *Idol with a Shell*, 1893. Musée d'Orsay, Paris.

The presence, to the left of Marie Angélique, of one of the ceramics inspired by pre-Columbian art that Gauguin created in large numbers in those years (another, though later example, is the *Idol with a Shell*) is a kind of "second signature" of the artist. The object assumes the value of a totem, of a primitive idol that bestows a mysterious and almost sacred atmosphere on the work, accentuated by the way the woman's hands are joined, as if in prayer.

Vincent van Gogh
(1853 - 1890)
The Bedroom

oil on canvas
22.6 x 29.1 in / 57.5 × 74 cm
1889

Van Gogh wrote to his brother Theo: "only here color [...] is to be suggestive here of rest or of sleep in general. In a word, looking at the picture ought to rest the brain, or rather the imagination [...]. The broad lines of the furniture again must express inviolable rest." In October 1888 he painted a first version of *The Bedroom* with such enthusiasm and he was so satisfied with the results ("I believe this bedroom to be my best work," he wrote to his brother in another letter) that he decided to replicate it in two more canvases; the one reproduced here is the third version, dating from the following year. The painter's words make it clear that his principal concern was not realistic representation. He used forms and colors to express what he felt and what he wanted to communicate to others: he was not at all interested in what he called "stereoscopic reality," i.e. the photographically exact reproduction of the subject in front of him. In order for his painting to express what

he felt, Van Gogh altered the colors and transformed the appearance of things to the point of distorting them. Thus, in depicting his own room he set out to convey an atmosphere of warmth and familiar security, a sign of the great importance he attached to his new home in Arles, where he intended to set up a "Studio of the South" in which to work alongside Émile Bernard and Paul Gauguin on the creation of a new kind of painting. Gauguin joined him there that same October of 1888, but the great difference in the temperaments of the two artists was the cause of continual conflict, and the experiment came to a tragic conclusion. For Van Gogh the new bedroom also provided him with a refuge after his work, "always exhausting and demanding, both mentally and spiritually," and so represented a great step forward with respect to the places where he had lived previously, "inns or boarding houses of the lowest sort," in which he had "lost any sense of order and the authenticity of life."

In *The Bedroom* Van Gogh tried to obtain the same combination of decorative effect and fluid and dense brushwork that he had sought in *Sunflowers*. The artist, who was to take the brilliance of his yellows to the point where he even used them to depict the sun, laid the paint directly on the canvas, in thick layers and with firm brushstrokes, creating an effect that has a powerful visual impact on the observer.

▶ **VINCENT VAN GOGH,** *Sunflowers*, 1888. Neue Pinakothek, Munich.

The deliberately simple furnishings of the room are not represented in a descriptive or anecdotal way: Van Gogh uses the few pieces of furniture to underline the atmosphere of human warmth he found in the bedroom, in the wooden double bed that conveyed a sense of familiar intimacy, "a feeling of solidity, of permanence, of tranquility, and it doesn't matter if I have to use bigger sheets when I make it."

In a letter to his sister Willemien, Van Gogh told her that the raison d'être for this canvas was the ambitious use of color: the three pairs of complementary colors (red and green, yellow and violet, blue and orange), along with back and white, producing an effect of great compositional daring. To give the picture greater chromatic equilibrium and balance the strong and bright colors, he advised his brother Theo to put it in a white frame, in order to emphasize the white present in the canvas.

Vincent van Gogh
(1853 - 1890)

Portrait of Doctor Gachet

oil on canvas
26.8 x 22.4 in / 68 × 57 cm
1890

An eccentric spirit, with a passion for art and an amateur painter himself, Dr. Gachet had had close ties with the artistic circles of Paris in his youth. In particular he had made friends with Paul Cézanne and Camille Pissarro, becoming their patron and collecting their work. An army doctor and major in the national guard during the Franco-Prussian War, he had bought a fine house on a hill above the valley of the Oise, where he went to live with his ailing wife and two children while continuing to practice in Paris, spending three days a week with his family.

It was he, in June 1890, who took in Van Gogh when he was discharged from the mental asylum at Saint-Rémy.

At Auvers-sur-Oise his friend lavished care and attentions on him, but above all he admired his painting: struck by the portraits the painter had brought with him, he ardently desired to have one of his own. In any case Van Gogh, constantly in financial difficulties and unable to bear having always to depend on his brother Theo for money, was happy to devote himself to portraiture, a genre which offered him an immediate gain and which he considered more marketable than landscapes or still lifes. However, his motivations for painting this portrait were not solely material, as it was linked to a precise intention, as Van Gogh explained in a letter to his sister: "I should like to paint portraits which would appear after a century to people living then as apparitions. By which I mean that I do not endeavor to achieve this by a photographic resemblance, but by means of our impassioned expressions – that is to say, using our knowledge of and our modern taste for color as a means of arriving at the expression and the intensification of the character." In this portrait the artist sought to capture, as he wrote to Gauguin, "the heartbroken expression of our time," a state of despair for which the medicinal herbs that Dr. Gachet holds in one hand represent both a hope and a consolation.

◄ **Vincent van Gogh,**
Portrait of Madame Ginoux
(L'Arlésienne), 1888.
Musée d'Orsay, Paris.

Thinking he could
attract possible clients by
showing them portraits he
had already painted, Van
Gogh brought several of
them with him to Auvers,

including the *Portrait of*
Madame Ginoux, known
as *L'Arlésienne*. It displays
strong similarities to the
portrait of Dr. Gachet:
the sitter's gloomy
expression, the bright
coloring of the abstract
background and the
decorative stylization.

In Gachet's hands
– represented in a paler
colorthan the face,
like "the hands of
an obstetrician" –

he has placed flowers
of digitalis, a medicinal
plant that alludes
to his profession of
homeopathic physician.

◀ **Vincent van Gogh,**
Mademoiselle Gachet in the Garden, 1890.
Musée d'Orsay, Paris.

At Auvers Van Gogh painted the world around him without focusing on particular themes as he had done previously: he passed from portraits of members of the Gachet family, whom he had no difficulty in persuading to sit for him (*Mademoiselle Gachet in the Garden*), to still lifes and landscapes of various kinds.

▶ **Vincent van Gogh,**
Church at Auvers, 1890.
Musée d'Orsay, Paris.

The *Church at Auvers*, viewed from the apse with its beautiful Gothic stained-glass windows, has a deep blue background, similar to that of the portrait of Dr. Gachet. Van Gogh painted them in the same days, under the impulse of powerful emotions.

GEORGES SEURAT
(1859 - 1891)

The Circus

oil on canvas
73 x 60 in / 185.5 × 152.5 cm
1890 - 1891

The Salon des Indépendants to which Georges Seurat sent *The Circus* opened on March 20, 1891. On March 29 the artist died at the age of just thirty-two, of an incurable illness.

The first reviews were lukewarm, but what upset Seurat most was the unspoken judgment of the great artist Puvis de Chavannes, whom he saw pass by his picture without even stopping. In the short span of his life, Seurat, a cerebral, cultured and sophisticated artist, made a decisive attempt to go beyond the "romantic" immediacy of impressionism, developing a method of painting based on precise scientific laws and revolutionizing the very concept of figurative art. In fact the central problem that he raised, in an age of positivistic veneration of the exact sciences, was to find an accord between art and science, and more precisely between painting and the physiology and psychology of perception.

Seurat's theory of painting was founded on optics, and it was accompanied by a scientifically developed technique, known as pointillism or divisionism: since light is the product of the combination of several colors, the equivalent of light in painting should result from the juxtaposition of colored dots that, viewed from a certain distance, re-create the unity of the tone and render the vibration luminous. Hence the highly geometric shapes of the figure in *The Circus* (depicted with accents of caricature, halfway between the embittered and the amused) and the sobriety of the colors and style are the result of a purely scientific conception of painting. On the other hand, this "pictorial testament" of Seurat has also been seen as a metaphor for the role of the artist who, personified by the clown in the foreground, reveals the ruthless mechanisms of society, clearly represented by the audience seated in different rows in accordance with their social rank.

The Circus is conceived wholly in terms of lines and areas of color, without any concern for the third dimension. The perspective in the composition is multiple and tends to flatten the space into a single plane: the spectators are arranged on parallel rows with no depth, and the horse's legs are foreshortened in two directions that are incompatible in reality, from the top down and the bottom up.

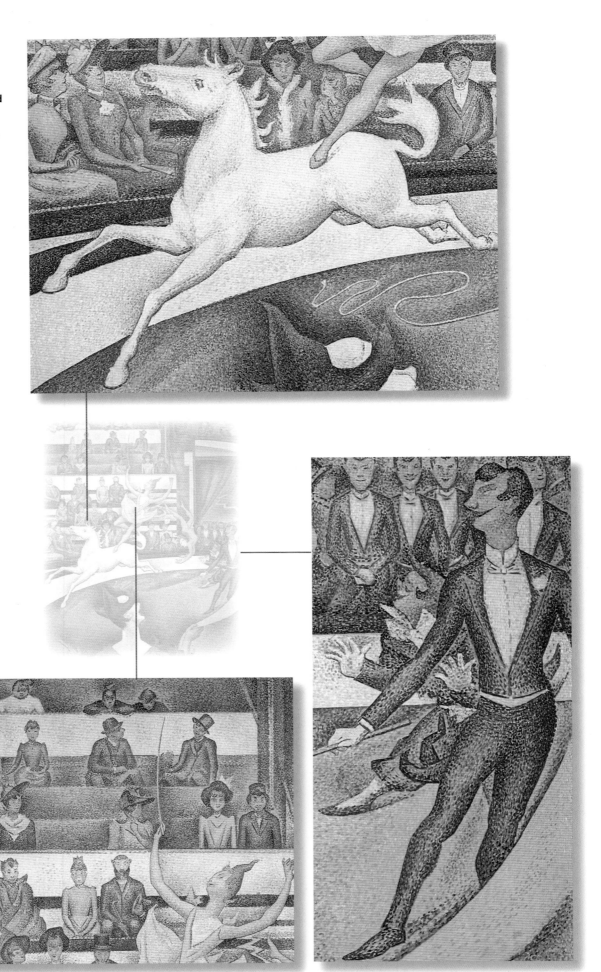

We know that the scene is meant to be set in the Cirque Fernando, a particular favorite of painters and located not far from Seurat's studio. But the real circus is not recognizable, and neither the rider nor the tamer are represented as individuals, but as anonymous silhouettes.

The Card Players

oil on canvas
18.7 x 22.4 in / 47.5 × 57 cm
c. 1890 - 1895

This is how Paul Cézanne explained his decision to go into voluntary exile at Aix-en-Provence, the city of his birth, after a long time spent in Paris: "I had resolved to work in silence until the day when I could defend theoretically the result of my efforts." In his youth, in fact, the painter had frequented the Parian cafés where the impressionists used to hang out, affecting fairly uncouth manners, an exaggerated southern accent and a deliberately unkempt appearance. In those years his works were derided and accused of clumsiness, owing to the way he spurned every academic rule in their execution and the fact that they reflected a fundamental objective on the artist's part: that of "starting again from scratch," ignoring the gains made by tradition, as if no one had ever painted before him, and solving problems of composition and color that he found interesting in a wholly new and personal way.

The prices of Cézanne's pictures started to rise slowly from 1899 onward, but at Aix people still saw him as the son of a wealthy banker who could permit himself an indulgence in harmless fantasies. However, his solitary life was often interrupted by the visits of his increasingly numerous followers, who regarded him as a sort of "savage" who had been able to find a completely different approach to the world of painting. He advised the young Émile Bernard to "treat nature by means of the cylinder, the sphere, the cone, everything brought into proper perspective," and to another youthful painter he confided his attempt to "represent perspective solely with the means of color." And this is, in fact, the way he handles the color and structure of a painting like *The Card Players*, in which the tension between vibrations of light and figures defined in geometric shapes finds a balance through the solid and highly "constructive" brushwork.

The position and
gestures of the figures
are perfectly symmetrical
and no attempt is made
to render the faces
psychologically expressive.
Their relationship is
wholly determined
by the opposition of
geometric forms and by
the equilibrium of the
luminous vibrations.

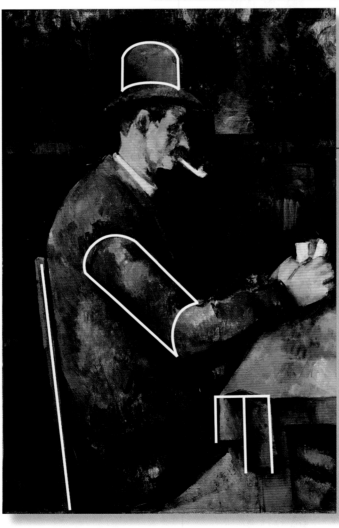

The fixity of the player
waiting for his partner
to make a move, for
example, is defined by
the cylindrical shape of
the hat, which is echoed
in the sleeve, by the
straight line of the back
of the chair and by the
tablecloth that hangs
straight down on his
side and is folded at an
angle on the other. The
psychological mutability

of the other player
is conveyed through
the paler colors of his
clothes, which catch
more of the light,
and by the less rigid,
softer character of his
features. The whole
is united and brought
back into balance by
the light and the way in
which the surfaces react
to it, creating a cozy
atmosphere.

PAUL GAUGUIN
(1848 - 1903)

On the Beach (Women of Tahiti)

oil on canvas
27.2 x 36 in / 69 x 91.5 cm
1891

Gauguin wrote in his memoirs: "If I were to tell you I am descended on my mother's side from a Borgia of Aragon, Viceroy of Peru, you will say it is not true and that I am merely being conceited." There was actually an element of truth in this claim: his mother did come from a distinguished family of the Peruvian nobility. He spent his early childhood with her in Lima and, after his move to Paris, the quest for his own origins, real or mythical, turned him into an indefatigable traveler, wandering between Brittany and the islands of the Lesser Antilles.

In 1891 the relative success of the auction of his paintings allowed Gauguin to set sail for Tahiti. Here he was fascinated by the indolent beauty of the local women, with their sturdy shoulders and broad hips. He represented them repeatedly in his pictures, from different angles and in various attitudes, but without giving them an identity of their own, and without any attempt at portraiture or realism.

In this canvas, the pronounced features of the faces of the two women on the beach call to mind primitive masks, or the ceramic masks and small wooden idols that the artist created in those years. In so-called "primitive" cultures (the Tahitian and pre-Columbian ones, but also those of Brittany and Japan) Gauguin sought the innocence of vision lost by Western art, now a slave to academic conventions, to space represented in perspective, to the realistic representation of the world. So he created a sort of new and exotic mythology: by isolating the two women (although in reality it was the same model who posed for both figures) on a flat surface with strong contrasts of color, he bestowed on them an impassive monumentality, transforming them into two primitive deities, seated on the fertile ground of a new Garden of Eden.

The painter is not so much interested in showing the two women engaged in a precise activity (although the figure on the right is plaiting palm fibers) as in constructing a decorative (and so not at all realistic) image in which all the elements – from the women's brightly colored clothing to the yellow sand and the red and yellow ribbons in their hair – balance each other in an overall chromatic harmony. The ocher-colored beach seems to be tilted toward us and even the background (the curved lines of the waves) creates no sense of space: the flat color is purely decorative, without any intention of conveying an impression of perspective.

▶ **Édouard Manet,**
At the Beach, 1873.
Musée d'Orsay, Paris.

The theme of figures
relaxing on the beach
had already been tackled
some twenty years earlier
by Édouard Manet in his
painting *At the Beach*,
which Gauguin may
have seen when it was
exhibited in Paris in 1884.
The basic conception of
the two works is similar,
but the way that the
space and colors are
handled is completely
different: in Manet's
picture perspective
is used to create
an illusion of space
stretching to the far
horizon, where some
boats can be seen; in
Gauguin's, on the other
hand, space is absent,
giving the image its look
of a pure, flat decoration.

▼ **Paul Gauguin,** *Soyez
mystérieuses (Be Mysterious)*,
1890. Musée d'Orsay, Paris.

The wooden bas-relief
Soyez mystérieuses, one
of the most significant
of Gauguin's pre-Tahitian
period, shows the degree
to which the artist wished
to return to the freshness
of the so-called primitive
arts. Carved in Brittany in
1890, the work reflects
the influence of pre-
Columbian art and the
taste for the undulating
line typical of art nouveau.

Alphonse Daudet and His Daughter

oil on canvas
35.4 x 45.9 in / 90 × 116.5 cm
1891

The writer Alphonse Daudet (1840-97), subject of this portrait by Eugène Carrière, loved humanity. He took an interest in the fate of human beings with a curiosity that was tinged with tenderness. For him, writing was chiefly a matter of describing encounters, personalities and experiences. His works are always inspired by reality, but he cannot be regarded as a naturalistic writer in the full sense of the word. He adds a touch of the marvelous to facts, not limiting himself to reporting them, but relating them through the filter of his own memory, and the warmth of his own feelings. His friendship with the painter Carrière developed toward the end of his life when, suffering from a disease for which his son Léon treated him with repeated injections of morphine, he was sketching his last characters.

In a letter dating from the year in which this portrait was painted, the painter revealed to Daudet how much their friendship had enriched him: "Such meetings – so rare, unfortunately! – uncover something of the line of the horizon [...] you have given me, dear Daudet, the sensation of this fullness."

Portraying his friend together with his daughter Edmée in 1891, Carrière seems to have resorted to the same "evocative" procedure in painting as Daudet used in his short stories, of which the artist was an enthusiastic reader. A past master at portraying the intimacy of the family, here he uses dark shadow to convey a sense of the veil of memory, or of impending death, out of which emerge the figures, the suffering expression of the writer and the childish one of his daughter. His painting is the fruit of a visual sensitivity taken to extremes: just as Monet trained his retina to analyze the most dazzling sunlight, Carrière accustomed his to darkness, allowing his figures to surface from it like apparitions. His portrait of father and daughter captures the appearance of a moment in an image that is not fully revealed, depicting an instant of intimacy, a fleeting contact between the visible and the invisible.

▶ **MEDARDO ROSSO,** *Ecce Puer (Behold the Child)*, 1906. Galleria d'Arte Moderna, Piacenza.

Carrière had in common with Auguste Rodin and Medardo Rosso an intense interaction between painting and sculpture: their forms which emerged out of the formless broke the rules, with their "unfinished" and "blurred" state, of the traditional artistic genres. In Rosso's *Ecce Puer*, for example, we find the same predilection for the representation of childhood and the atmospheric effects of which Carrière was fond.

In the intensity of the chiaroscuro, which emphasizes the faces and their expressions through pure effects of light and shade, Carrière's technique is highly original: there are no contemporary parallels to it, and it is necessary to go back to Rembrandt, and to his self-portraits in particular, to find an equivalent.

In this double portrait, the imbalance created by the oblique attitude of the father is softened by the frontality of the daughter. But it is the faces and gestures of the two sitters that attracts our attention more than their barely perceptible figures.

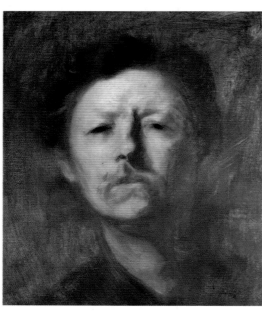

◀ **EUGENE CARRIERE,** *Self-Portrait*, 1893. Galleria degli Uffizi, Florence.

Carrière represents his own face as an apparition on the canvas, an effect that is reminiscent of the image on St. Veronica's kerchief.
The monochromatic background is painted in concentric brushstrokes that accentuate the sense of sudden appearance and equally sudden disappearance.

CLAUDE MONET
(1840 - 1926)

Rouen Cathedral, the West Portal and Saint-Romain Tower, Full Sunlight, Harmony in Blue and Gold

oil on canvas
41.73 x 28.74 in / 106 × 73 cm
1892 - 1893

In October 1890 Monet wrote: "I'm hard at it, working stubbornly on a series of different effects [...] the further I get, the more I see that a lot of work has to be done in order to render what I'm looking for: 'instantaneity,' the 'envelope' above all." These words clearly indicate the objectives pursued by the painter in his pictures painted "in series" between 1890 and 1900. To study the subjects he chose – whether they were haystacks, poplars, cathedrals or water lilies – in depth he painted them at different times of day: it is almost as if Monet, extremely sensitive to the tiniest variations in light and atmosphere with shifts in the dimensions of space and time, wanted to take snapshots of them, creating what to his contemporaries appeared to be, as a whole, an extraordinary poem on nature and to us today look individually like sequences from a movie. In February 1892 Monet went to stay in Rouen, setting up his studio in the front room of a dressmaker's shop: from there he could view the cathedral at an angle,

the best perspective from which to see the magical effects produced by sunlight on the façade. During the three months he spent in the city he was often racked by serious doubts over the outcome of the enterprise. In a letter to Alice Hoschedé he even admitted to having nightmares about the cathedral: "It fell on me [and] seemed to be pink or blue or yellow." After a period of inactivity, the painter returned to Rouen the following year: again he set to work tirelessly, on as many as eight canvases at once, but it was not until the May of 1895 that he was satisfied with the results and exhibited twenty of the thirty pictures in the series, which proved an enormous success. Georges Clemenceau, among others, wrote an article filled with praise, inviting the president of the republic Félix Faure to go to see the paintings and to purchase them for the good of the nation, as "together they represent a fundamental moment for art, a fundamental moment for humanity, a revolution carried out without firing a shot."

The canvases that make up the series, now dispersed among museums in various parts of the world (the Musée d'Orsay possesses five of them, but there are others in Washington, Boston and New York) analyze the effect created every day by the play of sunlight over the façade of the cathedral. In the early hours of the morning, as we see in *Rouen Cathedral, Morning Light*, the sun rises from behind one of the towers like a golden apparition, giving the church a well-defined outline; after gradually enveloping the pinnacles, the sunlight spills over onto the façade (*Rouen Cathedral at Dawn*), illuminating it more and more until the whole structure glows in the early afternoon (*Rouen Cathedral, Full Sunlight*). The shadows then spread from the square and the spires catch the last rays of the sun at sunset (*Rouen Cathedral, Evening*).

While working on the series, Monet had periods of disorientation in which he seemed to lose faith in what he was doing: at one point he wrote to Alice Hoschedé begging her not to see his pictures as "nothing but an obstinate jumble of colors." Judging by traditional criteria, it was true: his pictures are dazzling visions, in which the attempt to render the atmospheric effects of sunlight on the surface of the cathedral prevails over the exact definition of the architectural forms. See the towers, for example, in which there are no lines to convey their structural solidity and the subject is represented solely through color.

▲ **CLAUDE MONET,** *Rouen Cathedral, Morning Light*, 1894. Musée d'Orsay, Paris.

▼ **CLAUDE MONET,** *Rouen Cathedral at Dawn*, 1894. Musée d'Orsay, Paris.

▼ **CLAUDE MONET,** *Rouen Cathedral, Evening*, 1894. Pushkin Museum, Moscow.

Henri Rousseau
(1844 - 1910)

War

oil on canvas
44.9 in x 41.3 in /114 × 105 cm
1894

In 1894 Henri Rousseau, commenting on his most ambitious work, declared "War. It passes, terrifying, leaving despair, tears and ruin everywhere." The previous year the self-taught painter, a tax collector in the Paris toll office (a post that earned him the nickname Le Douanier, "The Customs Officer"), had given up his job in order to devote himself entirely to art. His mediocre and ordinary life contrasts with the pictorial universe he created, with his inexhaustible fantasy and highly original style. Equally surprising are his admiration for the academic painters of the Salon (Cabanel, Bouguereau, Gérôme) and the distance he maintained from the impressionists, to whose generation he belonged, especially if we consider that the first enthusiastic appreciation of his work came from important exponents of the avant-garde like Robert Delaunay, Guillaume Apollinaire, Georges Braque and Pablo Picasso. The latter held a banquet in honor of Rousseau in his studio in 1908: fascinated by the exuberance and sincerity of Le Douanier's vision, Picasso recognized in him the epitome of the naive painter, who was able to take the ingenuous approach of a primitive, as if he were the first man to hold a brush in his hand and had not been preceded by millennia of art history. The process of mythicizing, i.e. of going beyond a rational understanding of time and space, was fully realized in War, also known as Discord on Horseback. The image – inspired by the Franco-Prussian War of 1870 in which the painter played very little part – is created without recourse to anecdotal or narrative elements: the female figure glides above a bleak landscape, strewn with corpses, none of them wearing military uniform. Thanks to his extraordinary imagination, his clear use of line and an almost frozen light, Rousseau succeeded in creating a work with a powerful impact, illustrating a tragedy of every age.

◀ **THÉODORE GÉRICAULT,**
Epsom Derby, 1821.
Musée du Louvre, Paris.

The personification of war is a figure with simian features astride a bizarre animal that is half horse and half anteater, galloping through the air: this posture, used earlier by Théodore Géricault in the *Epsom Derby*, is deliberately deformed, and improbable in reality. War is not depicted by the narration of a historical event, but through the evocation of an atmosphere in which crows are feeding on human corpses; the land is arid and dark and the clouds are red. The choice of colors is symbolic: green, signifying hope, is absent; instead the picture is dominated by black and red, the colors of grief and blood that, with the white of the robe worn by the central figure, make up the German imperial flag.

◄ **HENRI ROUSSEAU,**
The Snake Charmer, 1907.
Musée d'Orsay, Paris.

The Snake Charmer,
a work painted
subsequently by the artist,
constitutes in this sense a
sort of companion piece
to *War*. Here he presents
an enchanted world.
peopled with exotic plants
and animals, in which
greens and yellows are the
dominant shades: a joyful
image, in which Rousseau
shows his talent for the
fantastic.

► **EUGÈNE DELACROIX,** *Liberty
Leading the People*, 1830.
Musée du Louvre, Paris.

The woman's pose derives
from a stereotype of
classical statuary, imitated
several times in the 19th
century, for example by
Eugène Delacroix, who
represents republican
values in the central figure
of *Liberty Leading the
People*, victorious thanks
to the sacrifice of those
whom we see lying dead
at her feet.

HENRI DE TOULOUSE-LAUTREC
(1864 - 1901)

The Moorish Dance

oil on canvas
112.2 x 121.1 in / 285 × 307.5 cm
1895

On April 6, 1895, the dancer known as "la Goulue" wrote to Toulouse-Lautrec, asking him to paint two panels to be set on either side of the entrance to her booth at the Foire du Trône, where she, her popularity now fading, was to perform the belly dance. In this letter she told the painter: "My dear friend, I will come to you on April 8, at two in the afternoon; my booth will be at the Trône, on the left as you enter; I have an excellent place and would be very happy if you had time to paint me something." La Goulue ("The Glutton") was the nickname of the Alsatian washerwoman Louise Weber, who had become a dancer and actress famous for her insatiable appetite and frenzied dances, especially the *quadrille naturaliste* (derived from the celebrated cancan) that was the principal attraction at the Moulin Rouge from 1890 onward. In 1895, grown fat and tired, she went into a sad decline that would see her become a flower seller at the Casino and a wrestler, animal tamer and fat lady at fairs. After living in a shantytown and working as a drudge in a brothel, she died in 1929, the same year as the two canvases painted by Toulouse-Lautrec, which she had immediately resold, entered the collections of the Louvre.

The famous dancer is depicted in the act of doing a high kick in her celebrated version of the cancan, in front of an audience that includes portraits of some of the painter's friends and fellow lovers of nightlife. With the unusual device of representing figures from behind in the foreground, he seems to be inviting passersby to stop and join the painted audience.

By displaying his works on the walls of public places, the artist gave back his painting – which was certainly not created for museums – its original decorative function, reaching a different, and to a great extent nocturnal, public that was in some ways more open-minded than the one that frequented the Salons or the private galleries of art dealers.

Seated at the piano is the photographer Paul Sescau, while his friend Maurice Guibert, in profile, watches the performance with evident interest. And then we can recognize, on the far left, the silhouettes of Gabriel Tapié de Celeyran (the painter's cousin), rubbing shoulders with the massive frame of Oscar Wilde, the dancer Jane Avril in a feathered hat, Toulouse-Lautrec himself with a derby on his head, as always out of scale (he was not quite five feet one inch tall) and the critic Félix Fénéon, with his angular profile, often mistaken for the dancer Valentin.

The only figures in the picture that justify its title of *The Moorish Dance* are the man wearing a turban and the woman playing the tambourine and dressed as an odalisque: La Goulue is still shown in the pose and costume that had made her celebrated as a dancer in the cabarets of Paris. The execution is very rapid and sketchy, limited to outlining the shapes of the figures in the background, left as usual in an unfinished state; artificial lights gleam on this yellowish surface and a crescent moon is visible through the window.

◄ **HENRI DE TOULOUSE-LAUTREC,** *Dance at the Moulin Rouge*, 1895. Musée d'Orsay, Paris.

In the second panel, placed on the left of the entrance to the booth, the painter represented the *Dance at the Moulin Rouge*, harking back to La Goulue's glory days in the dance halls of Montmartre with her partner Valentin, portrayed with the loose-limbed and caricatural traits that earned him the nickname of Le Désossé ("the Boneless").

Auguste Rodin
(1840 - 1917)
Balzac

plaster
118.1 x 47.2 in / 300 × 120 cm
1897

In the face of the chorus of criticism and condemnation provoked by the first exhibition of his work to the public of Salon in 1898, Auguste Rodin defended his statue of Balzac with pride: "This work, derided and mocked because it cannot be destroyed, is the result of the studies I've been carrying out all my life, the true goal of my aesthetic convictions. I was a different man the day I finished it: my evolution was complete." In fact visitors had sneered at the sculpture, comparing it to "a cow," while the more refined among them had described it as "a snowman" or "a shapeless pile of lava." The story had begun in 1891, when Émile Zola, on behalf of the Société des Gens de Lettres (the most important literary institution in France after the Académie Française), commissioned from Rodin a monumental statue of the great novelist to be erected at a prominent location in Paris. By the time the work was finished, the society was already unhappy with the sculptor over the fact that he had not respected the deadline (the contract had called for it to be completed in eighteen months). In reality, Rodin had needed all this time to collect background information, studying Balzac's works, his habits and his character, and going to the city of his birth, Tours. There he had even gone so far as to ask a tailor who had worked for the writer forty years earlier to make a suit to his measurements. Rodin also got hold of an old daguerreotype that portrayed Balzac at half length, with the collar open to reveal his bull neck. And he had read the precise descriptions of the writer made by Lamartine (a man with "eyes of flame" and an "enormous body") and Théophile Gautier (a "gaze lit up with Rabelaisian mirth"). The result, a monumental figure, its trunk only cursorily worked in order to bring out the expression on the face, was rejected by the Société des Gens de Lettres: it was only in 1939 that Rodin's *Balzac* found a home on Boulevard Raspail.

▲ **AUGUSTE RODIN,** *The Burghers of Calais*, 1885-95. Westminster Hall, London.

Rodin had already experimented with the subordination of form to idea and to the expression of character, although not in such extreme terms, in the monument to

The Burghers of Calais. Here observers/passersby are involved in the individual and non-heroic suffering of each figure and the sculptural block is humanized by the passage of ordinary inhabitants of the town of Calais.

◀ **UMBERTO BOCCIONI,** *Development of a Bottle in Space*, 1912. Museum of Modern Art, New York.

The plastic vitality and simplification of form of Rodin's *Balzac* would be a source of inspiration for this sculpture by Umberto Boccioni, executed in 1912 on his return to Italy from a visit to Paris.

Giovanni Boldini
(1842 - 1931)

Portrait of Robert de Montesquiou-Fezensac

oil on canvas
63 x 32.3 in / 160 × 82 cm
1897

Handsome, wealthy and arrogant, the poet, art critic and above all refined dandy Count Robert de Montesquiou-Fezensac (1855-1921) was one of the leading figures in the Parisian drawing rooms of the Belle Époque. It was he who laid down the law in matters of conduct and taste, contributing to the acceptance of art nouveau by the elite. And it was he who introduced his friend Marcel Proust into the most exclusive circles, although not without a touch of condescension and subtle cruelty, for which the writer took revenge by portraying him in the unflattering guise of Baron de Charlus in *À la recherche du temps perdu* (*Remembrance of Things Past*). And in *À rebours* (*Against the Grain*), the novel regarded as the bible of the decadent movement, Joris-Karl Huysmans drew extensively on the personality of Montesquiou-Fesenzac in his characterization of its protagonist, the sophisticated aesthete Jean des Esseintes. So the count was an ideal subject for the Ferrarese artist Giovanni Boldini, who had been living in Paris since 1872 and had become the favorite painter of high society, portraying slender and ethereal women and refined exponents of fashionable life in rapid and vibrant brushstrokes. The portrait of Montesquiou, shown at the Salon de Printemps, attracted great admiration, but also salacious and sarcastic comments from the count's numerous enemies, who mocked him for the pose of refined indolence in which he had had himself painted.

The novelist and journalist Jean Lorrain, who detested both Montesquiou and Boldini, wrote: "This year Robert de Montesquiou has entrusted the task of reproducing his elegant silhouette to Monsieur Boldini [...] also known as the Paganini of Attire. [...] Poor Monsieur de Montesquiou takes communion before his cane [...] swooning before it as Narcissus might swoon before a mirror." And it was over the elegant walking stick with which he is portrayed in the picture that Montesquiou fought a duel with the writer Henri de Regnier, who had told him: "You'd look better with a fan." He was unaware, poor man, that Montesquiou carried that cane in memory of the writer and critic Edmond de Goncourt, to whom it had belonged. On the count's death, the stick was acquired by an equally "eccentric" figure, the artist Salvador Dalí.

◀ **GIOVANNI BOLDINI,**
*Portrait of Madame
Charles Max*, 1896.
Musée d'Orsay, Paris.

Giovanni Boldini
was a past master at
representing the fleeting
splendor of the *fin-de-
siècle* generation, with its
mincing ways and guile.
Some of his portraits
are in stiff and formal poses, but more often,
as in his famous pictures
of women, they are in
relaxed and spontaneous
attitudes: see for
example the seductive
appearance of Madame
Charles Max, swathed
in a white evening dress
to which Boldini's rapid
brushstrokes impart glints
of moonlight.

▶ **HENRI DE TOULOUSE-LAUTREC,**
Portrait of Louis Pascal, 1891.
Musée Toulouse-Lautrec, Albi.

Montesquiou was one
of the best-known
dandies of his day, but
not the only one. The
same exquisite elegance
and refined dress can
be seen, for example, in the portrait of the
highly fashionable Louis
Pascal, painted a few
years earlier by Toulouse-
Lautrec. In fact Pascal, like
Montesquiou, Oscar Wilde
and Beau Brummell, had
made the quest for beauty
and elegance the principal
goal of his life.

The portrait of Montesquiou emphasizes the count's refined profile, his slim and arched silhouette, the meticulous but nonchalant elegance of his attire and his tapering fingers accentuated by the walking stick, held with as much delicacy as if it were a violin. The pose is the affected one typical of the fashionable portrait, a genre much in demand in the drawing rooms of Paris.

FÉLIX VALLOTTON
(1865 - 1925)

Child Playing with a Ball in the Corner of a Park

oil on cardboard mounted on wood
18.9 x 24 in / 48 × 61 cm
1899

In his diary the Swiss painter Félix Vallotton jotted down statements that are true declarations of intent: "I dream of a painting detached from any literal appearance of nature. I would like to reconstruct landscapes with the sole aid of the emotion they have produced in me, a few grand evocative lines and one or two details, chosen without false notions of accuracy, time or illumination." This was, in short, a renunciation of the realistic representation of nature, something which Vallotton had in common with the Nabis group, and a return to the classical tradition. The approach of the impressionists, passively dependent on sense data, on the light and the time of day, now appeared to have been superseded by the Nabis avant-garde of the 1890s, who sought to replace it with a rational and simplified vision. In this context Vallotton chose to express himself in black and white, without intermediate shades, in the woodcuts that made him famous and which help us to understand the uniqueness of his painting. The two different media of wood engraving and painting were interwoven in the development of a severe, terse style, based on two-dimensional images clearly defined by contrasts of color and of light and shade. The landscape in this picture is an example of this method, which he applied from the early nineties onward. The image is warm and at the same time seems to be frozen by a sense of superhuman calm: the scene of the child running after the ball in the silent limpidity of a sunny afternoon anticipates the metaphysical visions of Giorgio de Chirico, although the atmosphere is a far more relaxed one.

Even at a cursory glance it is apparent that something does not add up, as far as the rules of perspective are concerned, in the spatial arrangement of the painting. The foliage that fills the background constitutes a highly sculptural element, but one that is contradicted by the large expanse of sand in the foreground: here the running child is viewed from above, while the small female figures in the distance are represented frontally. It seems that the artist wanted to reproduce the slow movement of the eye along a curved axis that, by dividing the image into two different colored zones, pushes the figures and objects further back, toward the horizon.

And yet, notwithstanding the inconsistency of perspective, the equilibrium of the picture is not compromised: what lends harmony to the whole are the vivid contrasts of color, the tension between the large areas of flat color and the few strident touches, the yellows, the oranges, the white.

▲ **FÉLIX VALLOTTON,**
Dinner by Lamplight, 1899.
Musée d'Orsay, Paris.

▶ **FÉLIX VALLOTTON,**
The Poker Game, 1902.
Musée d'Orsay, Paris.

Vallotton is the painter of *Intimacy* (the title he gave to one of his series of woodcuts), scenes of bourgeois interiors in which what stand out are his terse vision and his attempt to capture the essence of every movement, like the authors of the Japanese prints of which he was so fond. Under the artificial light of a lamp we see a family gathered for a meal or a group of elderly men playing poker, in two works that are once again striking in their daring handling of space.

The Water Lily Pond: Harmony in Green

oil on canvas
35 x 36.8 in / 89 × 93.5 cm
1899

If he had not been a painter, Monet would probably have become a botanist. In this connection, one critic commented: "Monet reads more catalogues and pricelists of horticultural products than articles by aesthetes." In his youth, despite his financial problems, he always had a flower garden, and when he moved to Giverny in 1883, the first thing he did was to turn a kitchen garden filled with fruit and vegetables into one that he sowed with a range of plants chosen so that it would be continually in flower, from the early days of spring until the late fall. In 1890 his art finally began to achieve the success he had hoped for and the considerable amount of money he made from it allowed him to buy the house at Giverny and a plot of land with a pond in the middle that he turned into a water garden, a mysterious and exotic bit of paradise that was an inexhaustible source of subjects for the paintings of his last years. The roughly ten thousand square feet of the pond were soon surrounded by an artistic composition of flowers, trees and shrubs: the expanse of water was spanned by a wooden bridge in the Japanese style and filled with water lilies. Monet took refuge in his private universe at Giverny at one of the darkest moments in recent French history, the time of the Dreyfus case, which split the nation and induced many artists and intellectuals to take a political stand. But he seems to have withdrawn from the contemporary world to immerse himself in the Orientalizing Garden of Eden he had created: the result was the series of pictures of the so-called "Japanese bridge." In fact Monet admired the profound rapport the Japanese had with nature, which made them "a deeply artistic people." In 1904 he told a journalist a story that had impressed him: "A Japanese mason was building a wall and had placed a rose in front of him so that he could look at it every now and them and breathe in its scent while he worked. Don't you find that fascinating?" This was the kind of relationship with nature that Monet appreciated.

◀ **Utagawa Hiroshige,**
Inside Kameido Tenjin Shrine,
c. 1856. Private collection.

Monet had hung several
Japanese prints in his
dining room at Giverny,
which he liked to compare
with the water garden he
had created.
For example, the
"Japanese bridge" over
the lily pond, surrounded
by weeping willows,
echoes the one covered
with wisteria at the
Kameido Tenjin shrine,
depicted in a print by
Hiroshige.

 **Claude Monet,** *The Artist's
Garden at Giverny,* 1900.
Musée d'Orsay, Paris.

Monet's two gardens at
Giverny – the flower one
in front of the house and
the one with the water
lilies – were conceived as
complementary settings.
While the water garden
had an Oriental character,
the one planted with
flowers, depicted in *The
Artist's Garden at Giverny,*
was more traditional:
although not rigidly
symmetrical, it took its
inspiration from 18th-
century models.

▼ **Claude Monet,**
The Water-Lily Pond, 1904.
Musée d'Orsay, Paris.

In the 1920s, when one of his eyes was already clouded by a cataract, Monet went back to painting in his water garden, representing the water lilies in innumerable ambitious canvases of imposing size. Their composition was freer than in the series of the "Japanese bridge": it is no longer possible to distinguish the part of the flowers under water from the part above, and there are no more boundaries between water and sky.

GUSTAV KLIMT
(1862 - 1918)

Rose Bushes Under Trees

oil on canvas
43.3 x 43.3 in / 110 × 110 cm
c. 1905

The vivacious atmosphere of *fin-de-siècle* Paris corresponded, in Vienna, to the languid melancholy of the *finis Austriae*, the sunset of the Austro-Hungarian Empire. Between 1890 and the First World War the era of Franz Joseph sang its swan song amidst an extraordinary cultural richness that was accompanied by an awareness of its own dissolution. The anxieties of this declining golden age were expressed through the voices of Sigmund Freud, Ludwig Wittgenstein, Robert Musil, Gustav Mahler and Arnold Schoenberg: the entire generation seems to have shared the knowledge that it stood on a ground riddled with cracks, cracks that spread into the realms of the unconscious, of language, of the whole of reality. Art, in the person of Gustav Klimt, presented itself as a last metaphysics to cling to, a sort of new idolatry capable of creating a parallel world: for the style developed by Klimt really was a parallel language, one that served as the model of a symbolic transformation of the world. Klimt only began to paint landscapes in the years of his maturity, during the summers that he spent, from 1900 to 1916, in the peaceful lake setting of the Attersee with his companion Emilie Flöge. The artist worked in the open, setting up his easel among the trees or on a boat, just like Claude Monet, and yet the results attained by the two painters could not be more different. Klimt did not aspire to reproduce reality as he saw it, but to create a separate one, through a highly personal set of signs that distanced his work from the subject he had in front of him, stripping it of the spontaneity and immediacy characteristic of the impressionist landscape. A painting like *Rose Bushes under Trees* relies solely on the decorative effects created by the square format, which conveys a sense of calm and harmony, and by the colors, laid on in minute touches, like the tesserae of a mosaic. The overall impression is that of a wood filled with inner life and silence: time is suspended and the atmosphere is mysterious, owing to the exclusion of any sign of human presence, its place taken by an almost endlessly proliferating vegetation.

▼ **Gustav Klimt,**
Judith (or Salome), 1909.
Galleria d'Arte Moderna,
Venice.

The symbolic character
of Klimt's works is
highlighted by his
adoption of a style that
produced images of
women of an unsettling
sensuality, icons of a
Vienna reminiscent of
ancient Byzantium, which
placed eroticism at the
center of its existential
anxiety. Judith, with her
elongated shape and
markedly decorative
character, is an example
of the "eternal feminine"
idolized by Klimt to the
point of obsession.

▲ **Claude Monet,**
*The Garden of the Hoschedé
Family at Montgeron*, 1877.
Hermitage Museum,
St. Petersburg.

The dense mesh of colors

woven by Klimt is the
result of several sessions
in front of a landscape
similar, for example,
to the one that Monet
painted in *The Garden of*

*the Hoschedé Family at
Montgeron*: but where
the impressionist tried
to capture the luminous
and atmospheric effect
of a sunny afternoon,

Klimt, with his
two-dimensional
representation, creates
an image that is almost
symbolic, and wholly
decorative.

The foreground
expands to take up almost
the whole of the picture
and the line of the horizon
is very high: only in the
top right corner can a very
small patch of sky be seen.
The roses, which give the
painting its title, are barely
visible: the true subject
is color, which fills the
canvas, almost creating a
sense of claustrophobia.
The technique he used is
a pattern of small touches
of color, not pure as in
the pictures of the French
pointillistes, but mixed
in infinite gradations, as
in a mosaic. The vision is
fragmentary, as if focused
on the detail of a wood,
frozen and rendered
intense by a representation
that records neither
light nor shade, just the
eminently decorative value
of that piece of nature.

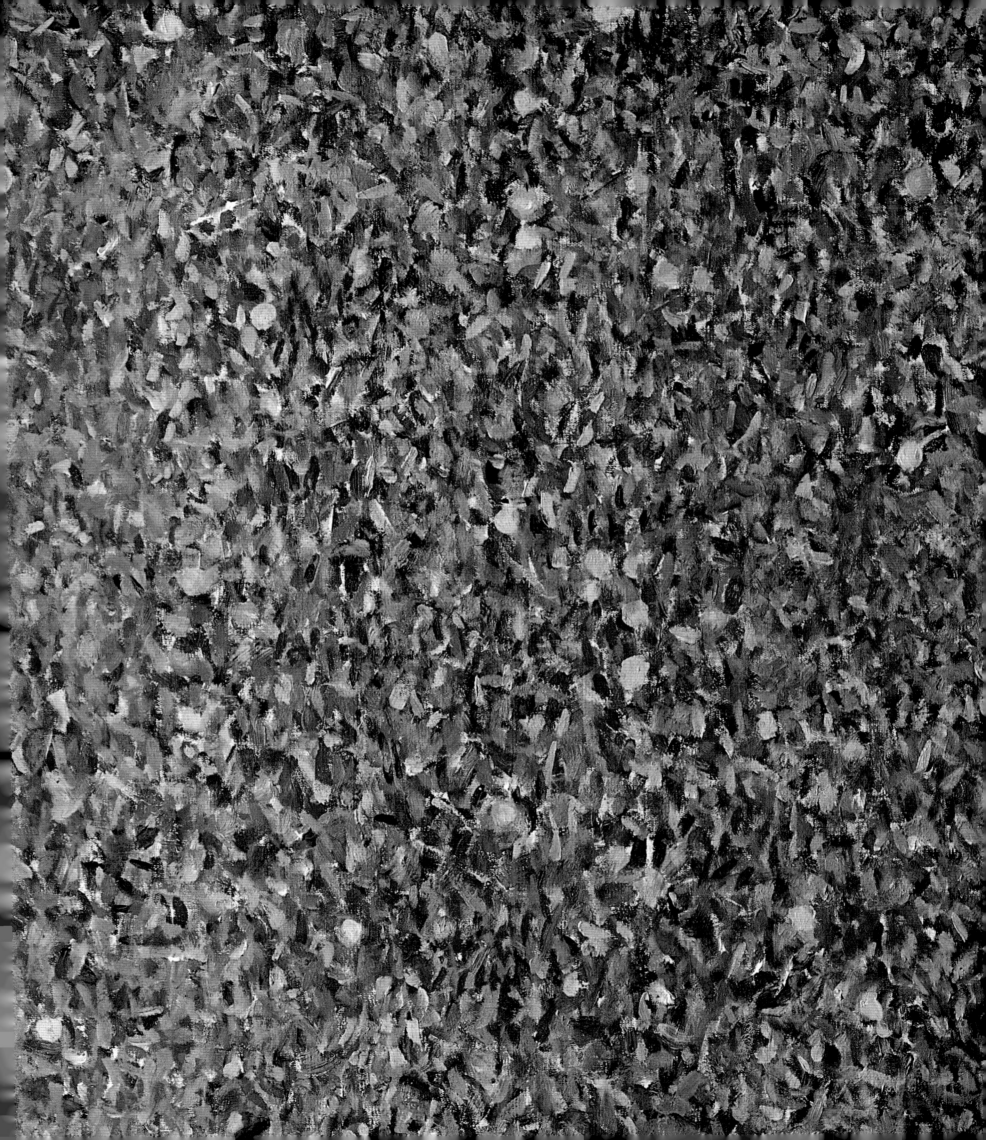

Index of Illustrations

Numbers in bold type refer to the pages where the masterpieces of the Orsay are analyzed individually